MU00900189

Endoi. _____

"Uduak Afangideh walked into our church almost five years ago and she 'took it by storm!' It was a God-storm full of love, joy, conviction, and truth. It took me by surprise! I had never seen anything quite like it. That is why I am so excited about her book. You will encounter a woman of God, writing about women of God, to inspire women of God. Don't be surprised when you are caught up in this wonderful storm!"

—**Buddy Bell**
Senior Minister
Landmark Church of Christ

"Uduak writes as led by the Holy Spirit. She captures your attention, then keeps it with her gift of Godly wisdom and insight into today's women. This well written book relates to women of all ages and is perfect for personal Bible studies and for ladies, small group studies. A must read."

—**Sherry DeBray**
Author
Desperate Christian Women and *The Teachers Gift*
Montgomery, Alabama

"This inspiring book by Uduak Afangideh is well-written and has much to offer to Christian sisters. I particularly like the way it deals with situations that most women have either endured or know someone that has endured the situation. We can all relate. This would be a good ladies' Bible study book. Let me know when it is published, and I will make sure to tell my home congregation."

—**Renee Andrews**
Author and Christian Novelist
published in
Mornings With Jesus 2014 – September 2013
Bride Wanted – July 2013
Profiled – February 2013
Heart of a Rancher – January 2013

"Uduak Afangideh has done a great job with this book. It was very encouraging, and I enjoyed reading it. Some stories made me cry like a baby. The idea of having questions nestled within each chapter made it easier to stop and reflect about each of the sections. I hope many get to read [this book]."

—Paula Harrington
Author
A *Common Bond* and *A Sunday Afternoon With the Preachers' Wives,*
Blogger and Speaker

Sister to Sister

Sister to Sister

INSPIRING STORIES OF HOW AN EXTRAORDINARY GOD TRANSFORMS ORDINARY WOMEN TODAY

Uduak Afangideh

Unless otherwise noted, all Scriptures are taken from the *Holy Bible, New International Version®, NIV®*. Copyright © 1973, 1978, 1984 by Biblica, Inc.™ Used by permission of Zondervan. All rights reserved worldwide. www.zondervan.com

Scripture references marked NKJV are taken from the *New King James Version*. Copyright © 1982 by Thomas Nelson, Inc. Used by permission. All rights reserved.

Scripture references marked NRSV are taken from the *New Revised Standard Version Bible: Anglicized Edition*, copyright 1989, 1995, Division of Christian Education of the National Council of the Churches of Christ in the United States of America. Used by permission. All rights reserved.

ISBN 13: 978-1-4954-0354-5
ISBN 10: 1-4954-0354-8
Library of Congress Catalog Card Number: 2014902658

Dedication

To my mother, Affiong Okon Mkpong (Eka Ini),
and my mother-in-law, Grace Thompson Afangideh (Nne).
Though you ladies are with the Lord, your stories live on in the
lives of those who share your heritage.

And to
Salem, Israel, and Elias—My story would be just another ordinary story without you guys in it.

Tribute

This book is a tribute to Grace Farrar,
who went to be with our Lord while it was in process.

Contents

Foreword

THERE IS NOTHING that promotes hope or joy more than realizing that the God of Heaven and Earth not only allows us, but desires for us to call him Father. When that wonderful truth takes root in our hearts, this hectic life gives way to peace. Our fears are replaced with faith, and grace steps in where doubts formerly ruled. Where once we were lonely sojourners in a dark world, our Father now calls us his chosen, holy, beloved children.

Family. What a powerful word in a world where it is so easy to feel alone. And regardless of whether we're separated by language, continents, or time, this community of believers that Christ has established is our catalyst for faith and encouragement. We must realize that church isn't a place we go a couple of times a week. Church is our family.

To be in Christ, places us in the midst of the greatest story ever told, God's story. From the beginning in a scenic garden, we watch as the first family deals with disobedience and grief and surely wonders why life turns out the way it sometimes does, leaving broken hearts along a weary path.

As we stroll through the Bible we encounter many others who, regardless of their trials and temptations, stand firm. They allow their love for a God who never fails to keep them on course.

Through his word, our Heavenly Father has shown us that our problems aren't original even though they may be to us. In fact, a wise writer once stated that nothing new was under the sun. Great encouragement comes from knowing that a family member has fought our battles and gained the victory.

This beautiful book by Uduak Afangideh is a portrait into the lives of precious women of faith. Walk with them down their roads of grief, heroism, and joy and allow their stories to come to life. Be inspired as you read how your sisters have prevailed despite their heartaches and allow their stories to cheer you on in your own journey. And then thank the Father who will never disappoint or abandon us and for those who have pressed on and finished the good fight.

May we strive to walk worthy of our calling while bringing others into this glorious family.

—**Paula Harrington**

Preface

THE BIBLE IS full of real life heroes, people who endured various hardships, but held on to their faith and were amply rewarded. Often, though, it appears we have heard those stories so many times that the characters appear larger than life. The fact that we know how the stories end also makes them appear more like fables than real-life stories. Living among us today, however, are Christian ladies who have faced many trials and tribulations, but like Bible heroes and heroines, they remain standing, strengthened in their faith, examples to all of us. It is my desire to present the stories of these ladies, not merely as biographical information but to show that the God of Bible times is still working in people's lives today. In so doing, I echo the words of Prophet Habakkuk who said, "LORD, I have heard of your fame; I stand in awe of your deeds, O LORD. Renew them in our day, in our time make them known" (Habakkuk 3:2 NIV 1984).

This book presents an in-depth look at ordinary women of today, women whose lives have been touched by an extraordinary God. The struggles they faced and the victories they won are highlighted in an attempt to encourage other Christian ladies in their daily walk with the Lord. This book is designed to be used as a Bible study material either for personal study sessions or for group discussions.

The review questions nestled within each chapter are designed to give additional insights and to provoke thought and application of the materials presented.

I believe that every woman today has a story to tell. My prayer is that we can see ourselves in the stories of these women and be encouraged to stand strong, knowing that as women, we are all facing similar battles on this journey of life. As these stories resonate within your Spirit, I hope you will let me know about your own experiences.

One last word: I know you are aware of other women who have spectacular stories to tell, so please contact me and by His grace, we shall soon be learning some valuable life lessons from their lives.

Acknowledgments

BEING AN AUTHOR has turned out to be one of the most exciting adventures of my life! In spite of many months of writer's block and thousands of miles of traveling within two continents to gather the stories told in this book, I am still overjoyed by this notion of sharing the stories of women today who have faced all odds and yet remain standing. I realize that this book would not have been possible without the guidance of the Holy Spirit and those whom He worked through to encourage me and to be a part of this journey.

I owe a debt of gratitude to: Stephanie Bell, the ideal minister's wife who heard this idea as it was being conceived and gave it wings; my wonderful life groups at the time who prayed weekly about this adventure and lifted me up; my father, whom I have always looked up to, the first one to believe in my childhood dreams of writing; my siblings and their families who encouraged me and shared my joys and my frustrations; my wonderful children who gave me the space I needed, even when it meant I was often distant and off in my own world; my husband, Peter, who has encouraged every desire of my heart and always given me wings to fly. These people carried me through the rough times, believed in me, and refused to allow this to be yet another unfinished project.

In the course of writing this book, the Lord has led my path to cross with those of wonderful Christian authors who have paved the path already, and I owe a debt of gratitude to Paula Harrington, Sherry Debray, and Renee Andrews, who shared their wisdom and experiences with me. My gratitude also goes to Katie Atchison, my wonderful in-house editor, to Kristin Payne, who allowed me to borrow her mind, and to the team at Winepress Publishers.

Finally, and most especially, to the women who have shared their stories with me, I say a big thank you. I feel highly honored that you not only gave me entrance into your world, but you gave me permission to share these stories with fellow travelers on this journey of faith. We cried together as these stories were told, and I still cry as I read them over and over again. You have been a true inspiration to me, and I pray that those who read your stories will draw strength from you and from our faithful God who waits to reward us all.

Introduction

THIS BOOK, ON the surface, may appear as a storybook meant solely to entertain, but when one looks deeper, it becomes obvious that it is actually a road map of the lives of various Christian ladies who have faced life's struggles and emerged victorious. The author has skillfully welded together the stories of these ladies to show the imperative principles that we all live by the choices we make, whether they be good or bad. The stories of the ladies in this book show that the choices made by us all, not only affect us, but often affect generations and nations. Perhaps nowhere else is this principle more evident than in the history of one of the ladies featured in this book, Grace Thompson, in Chapter Seven. This lady was chosen by the Lord to be my mother.

At the time Dad was killed by rebel Biafran soldiers during the Nigerian civil war, Mom was at the prime of her life. She was still as beautiful as ever, and there were at least three options open to her: she could have returned to her homeland in the neighboring Abia state and been assisted by family members in raising her sons; she could have remarried any of the dozens of eligible suitors who expressed interest in her; she could have rejected the first two options and chosen to stay in her marital home in a society that had no welfare scheme for widows or orphans and raise her boys by herself. Mom chose to endure hardship, rejecting the ease that would have accompanied either of the first two options. Mom (or Nne, as she was popularly called) was able, by that singular decision, to change the course of her children's future.

Another lady, Sister Grace Farrar, portrayed in Chapter Five, made the choice of leaving the ease and comfort of raising children in a developed and advanced American society to suffer the hardships of a developing country in the 1960's. This singular decision led to the establishment of the African Christian Hospital in Onicha Ngwa, in southeastern Nigeria, and the provision of world class health care to thousands of Nigerians. The love of the Lord reflected in her eyes as she lived among these people and led many to the Lord. Her name has become a household name in a continent far removed from her continent of birth. Yes, we are all governed by the choices we make daily.

Throughout the book, the author portrays women who battle with issues as grave as cancer and Parkinson's disease and as heartbreaking as barrenness and the unfaithful acts of husband and children. She shows how these women refused to allow difficult situations to define them, but rather made the choice to trust and honor God in their afflictions. She provides the details of each situation so that the reader is drawn into the stories and brilliantly depicts the faithfulness of God in every situation these ladies face. She makes the point that the faith of these ladies was strengthened by the choices they made.

Often, one blames fate, luck, favoritism, or predestination, failing to realize that the things that promise instant gratification or ease rarely endure, and the things that offer lasting satisfaction do not always appear appealing initially. Here, then, is the human dilemma, the dilemma of choice. Jesus calls it the narrow road. The right choice overturns what is commonly known as bad destinies, and a bad choice destroys all that is regarded as good fortune.

Let the Christian sister be reminded that she is a custodian of life. It is she who is the custodian of civilization and she who determines the pace of progress on this planet. Let her know that she holds the key of heaven for many souls as an ornament of glory. And if she would come to terms with this immutable principle, then the author's effort would have been bountifully rewarded.

I am grateful to the author for the privilege of saying a few words in this dialogue between Christian sisters.

—P.T. Afangideh

CHAPTER 1

Ordinary Women, Extraordinary God

Many women have done excellently, but you surpass them all.
—King Lemuel (Proverbs 31:29 NRSV)

ONE OF THE mysteries of Christianity is the fact that a Holy God can dwell in mere mortals and by that singular act transform those mortals into His image. When we come to God with all of our imperfections, believing in Jesus as Lord and Savior, He not only cleanses us from all sin, but imputes to us His righteousness. He takes our ordinary, everyday lives and makes us extraordinary in thought, words, and action. As Christian women, the roles we play in the lives of husbands, children, parents, siblings, and other relatives, make us exceptional and special. When God transforms us, He takes we who are mere clay and refines us until we become extraordinary wives, mothers, siblings, daughters, and workers in the kingdom.

In an attempt to fully understand what such an extraordinary woman would look like, I reached out to Christian sisters in different churches and asked for their concept of the word, extraordinary, as it applies to those whom they think this word describes. Their enlightening and inspired insights are presented below in the form of an acrostic:

Ex- The *extraordinary* woman is one that seeks to excel in all she does. She is not content to merely do it well, but constantly strives to do better. Far from being a perfectionist, she is aware of her failings, and rejoices in knowing she is called to a higher level of expectation than those around her. By striving for perfection, she keeps her eyes focused on Him alone, who makes her faith perfect (see Hebrews 12:1). She is quick to confess her shortcomings and quick to get back on her feet and keep trying. Because her eyes are fixed on the prize, it is easy for her to forget what is behind and press on to the goal ahead (see Philippians 3:14).

T- She is *trustworthy*, keeping the confidences of those who are part of her world. Surely, the heart of her husband trusts in her (see Proverbs 31:11), but so does the heart of others who know her. Before her, they can be themselves, not fearing condemnation or harsh judgment, for on her lips is the law of kindness. Not only does she guard her lips, but she is trustworthy with regard to finances and other treasures that are entrusted to her. She does not dwell in excess, but generously shares with all around her. She is faithful to God in her giving and teaches her household to do the same.

R- The extraordinary woman is *resourceful*. She looks around her and makes do with what is available. Like the virtuous woman, she does not depend on others to provide for her, but works willingly with her hands, creating a safe and happy haven for those in her world. She knows how to turn what looks like nothing into something special, be it creating a meal from leftovers or making a centerpiece from scrap material. She is constantly on the lookout for ways of improving herself and creative ways of using the resources around her. She is radiant because she does not allow the cares of this world to drag her down. Well aware of the dangers that abound in the world, she guards her heart, rejoicing in her redemption and seeking the redemption of the hurting and lost all around her.

A- She is an *accomplished* soul. Instead of comparing herself with those around her and seeing only her faults, she knows that she is wonderfully and fearfully made.

2

She rejoices in what God has done in her, through her, and by her. She sees herself through the eyes of her Maker and rejoices in who He has created her to be. Because every accomplishment brings her joy, she is able to rejoice in the accomplishments of those around her, generous in her praise and encouraging in her suggestions. She is alert and aware of her surroundings and the events going on around her. Not oblivious to the fact that we are in a spiritual battle on Earth, she constantly arms herself with the weapons of her warfare (see Ephesians 6:11-18) and is careful to be in prayer at all times.

O- She realizes that she is an *overcomer* and that the battle against the forces of the rulers of this world has already been won. Although still engaged in daily spiritual battles, she fights from a position of victory. This realization allows her to speak with authority, calling out the evil one when he appears to deceive, steal, kill, or destroy (see John 10:10), claiming the abundant life that has already been given to her and hers. She walks in obedience, submitting herself to the authority of her Lord and Master, denying herself those things that do not please the Lord, seeking only His will for her life. She lovingly submits to the authority of her husband, not lording it over him, but by her words, thoughts, or actions, she honors him in her heart and in her conversations with others (see 1 Peter 3:5-6).

R- The extraordinary woman is *resilient*. Though life throws her many curve balls and she often falls and stumbles, she has the ability to pick herself up and with her strength in the Lord, keep on going. Like the Apostle Paul, she can say that she has been "afflicted in every way, but not crushed; perplexed, but not driven to despair; persecuted, but not forsaken; struck down, but not destroyed" (2 Corinthians 4:8-9 NRSV). She is able to comfort others and empathize when they hurt because she has also experienced pain and hurt. She is able to sing through the dark, stormy nights for she knows that weeping may endure for the night, but joy does come in the morning (see Psalm 30:5).

D- She walks in *dignity*, with full realization that she is the daughter of the King. She is well aware of what is expected of her as one

3

who is royalty. Life does not cause her to slump her shoulders or hang her head down. She faces all challenges with the power of her authority as a princess, speaking with authority and calling things that are not, as if they were (see Romans 4:17). Well aware of her ability to destroy strongholds, she guards her heart and her mind, being always ready to reign over negative authority in her life and in her household (see 2 Corinthians 10:4).

I- She is an *intercessor*. Realizing the power that she has as a princess of God, she takes it upon herself to intercede on behalf of those in her life. She knows the power of prayer, believing in the promises of Him who said, "Call to me, and I will answer you, and show you great and mighty things, which you do not know" (Jeremiah 33:3 NKJV). Knowing full well that God is always looking for someone to stand in the gap (see Ezekiel 22:30), she readily and willingly intercedes for her husband, her children, and other members of her family. Every need, expressed or perceived, becomes a reason for prayer. She knows just how easy it is to promise to pray for someone and then, in the hustle and bustle of life, forget, so she keeps a prayer journal and records prayer requests. She is quick to offer "on the spot prayers" for those who express prayer needs and easily asks others what she needs to be in prayer about. Realizing that the life of an intercessor is often inconvenient, she consciously carves out time and specific places for prayers, often at the break of dawn or at midnight. Because she knows that some problems require more than prayers (see Mark 9:29), she is quite familiar with the concept of fasting and tarrying before the Lord.

N- She is *neighborly*. These days when people have thousands of friends on Facebook, but do not know the people next door, the extraordinary woman reaches out to her neighbors, taking the time to know them and to be involved in their lives. She not only talks to them across the fence, but visits them in their homes, sharing meals or baked goods. She watches out for them, inviting them into her home and into her life. Taking seriously the parable of the Good Samaritan, she realizes that anyone in her path is her neighbor, and so she is always on the lookout for opportunities to reach out and do good to all she meets. Her children's friends are not only welcome in her home, but she intentionally invites them over and plans activities with them in mind. Her husband's buddies find her home a haven, where they can stop by at any time and enjoy his company and a meal.

A- She is *agreeable* and *accommodating* and has a demeanor that welcomes all into her presence. She is quick to give people the benefit of the doubt and easily forgives. She is neither critical nor quick to condemn, but easily makes allowances for people's mistakes. Like the virtuous woman, she opens her mouth with wisdom and on her tongue is the law of kindness (see Proverbs 31:26). When she finds herself being critical or harsh, she is quick to confess and seek forgiveness, admitting her mistakes gracefully without apportioning blame.

R- The extraordinary woman is *righteous*. Realizing that her righteousness is of the Lord, she clings to Him, desiring to walk in purity and holiness. She daily looks to Him, knowing that her righteousness is by grace and through faith in the Lord Jesus Christ (see Romans 3:21-22). She lives a life of holiness, knowing that He who called her is holy and expects her to be holy in all she does (see 1 Peter 1:15). She is quick to confess her sins and seek forgiveness, but cautious not to continue in sin because of the grace that she readily receives from Him. She runs steadily the Christian race, knowing that there is a crown awaiting her in glory. She walks righteously before the Lord, striving for perfection, not out of fear, but motivated by love of the One who gave it all for her.

Y- She *yearns* to please God and yearns to spend eternity with her Father and loved ones who have gone on before her. Realizing that this fallen world is not her home, she lives with eternity in mind. She knows that her children will never love her enough for the sacrifices she makes for them, nor will her husband ever praise her enough to make up for all efforts. She does it all joyfully, knowing that her Father alone knows just how to reward her both on this earth and in eternity. Her goal is not to please her husband, children, boss, or parents, but to please Him. She longs to hear Him say, at the end of a rewarding life, "Well done, good and faithful [daughter]," and that will surely make it all worth it. And so her goal is to please Him daily, in word, thought, and actions.

If you are at all like me, this acrostic from my fellow sisters easily makes us feel much less than extraordinary. But far from being discouraged, it gives me something to aim for. As we begin this journey of studying the lives of today's extraordinary women, my prayer is that these stories will encourage us all and give us more reasons to keep on striving until we become all that He has called us to be.

CHAPTER REVIEW

1. Which of the words in the acrostic made you pause and re-evaluate the claim that we are all extraordinary by virtue of our femininity? Why?

_____

_____

_____

2. Which of the words in the acrostic poses the greatest challenge for you and why?

_____

_____

_____

3. What changes need to be made in your life and your daily routines for the above description of an extraordinary woman to describe you more fully?

_____

_____

_____

CHAPTER 2

Struggles With Infertility
(Though the Fig Tree Does Not Blossom)

God often brings us to a point where we have no choice but to admit that we need nothing else besides Him. It is when we arrive at that point and open wide our arms to embrace Him and Him only that He fills us to overflowing with our heart's desires.
—Kim

KIM WAS THE first child and the only girl in a family of three, born to traditional Christian parents in Montgomery, Alabama. From a very early age, she was aware of her parents' expectations of her, and she grew up to have the same expectations of herself—that of being a Christian wife and mother. Kim's mother and grandmothers set a high standard of what they thought a Christian lady should be—one given to hospitality, a keeper of the home, and an adept manager of her household. No one was surprised when Kim went to a Christian college and majored in home economics. It appeared that her parents' highest goal for her was to attend a Christian school, meet a good Christian man, and "settle down."

In Kim's junior year, those expectations were realized. She met a Bible major and married him twelve months later. When her husband landed a full-time job at a Christian university a year later, she knew the timing was right to start a family. Two years passed without conception, and Kim and her husband knew something was wrong. They consulted a fertility specialist who carried out various tests and exploratory surgery. Kim was diagnosed with endometriosis and unexplained infertility. Doctors began hormonal treatments and gave a hopeful prognosis of conception within a few months. The months dragged into years, and more aggressive tests were continuously carried out.

After five years of infertility, Kim and her husband opted for in vitro fertilization, fully believing that it would yield positive results. With each failed result, the stress on their marriage increased. "The way we handled the situation further highlighted our differences," Kim says. "I was more verbal in expressing my disappointment and viewed his silent reticence as indifference."

Not only did her marriage feel the strain of the infertility, her relationship with God was also affected. Kim recollects going through the full range of emotions spiritually. "I remember being mad and I remember pleading and bargaining. I doubted God's love for me, often feeling like a stepchild."

It didn't help matters at all that during that time it seemed like all of her friends were having babies. She was constantly attending baby showers or babysitting for her friends. Kim remembers asking over and over, "Why me, Lord?" Often she would fall on her knees and pray in desperation, "Lord you are the one who placed this desire for children in my heart. If you will not satisfy this desire, then please take it away."

The most disconcerting part of praying about this issue was that Kim never received answers and never felt peace in her heart after crying out to God about her infertility. Although she kept on with her Christian responsibilities in the church, especially as they related to her duties as a youth minister's wife, Kim reached a point where she could no longer pray about the issue. In hindsight Kim says, "I never reached a point during those years where I felt that if it was God's will for us to be childless that I could accept it. I kept on bargaining, questioning, and pleading. I felt that either God was not listening to me or He was telling me no, and I just did not want to accept 'No' as an answer."

Interestingly though, Kim's disappointment pushed her deeper into God's Word. She admits seeking Him more during those times. She often withdrew to be alone with Him, desiring to know why He was not granting her heart's desires, wanting more than anything else just to understand.

SECTION REVIEW

1. The Bible has stories of women who were infertile. They include Sarah, Hannah, Rebecca, Manoah's wife, Michal, the Shunammite woman, and Elizabeth. Divide these women into groups and carry out a brief study of two or three of these women under the following headings:

   a) Name
   b) Reasons for infertility (if given)
   c) Notable prayer or request during the period of infertility
   d) Length of infertility (if given)
   e) Age at conception (if given)
   f) Notable prayer or request after conception/delivery
   g) Name of child born at end of infertility
   h) Accomplishments of child born at end of infertility

Share the results of the group study in a group discussion.

2. Read God's promise to the barren woman in Psalm 113:9. Make a list below of women that you know personally, in whose life this promise has been fulfilled.

_____

_____

_____

Seven years into the infertility, Kim was almost thirty years old. She decided, out of despair, to consider adoption. She and her husband contacted Christian Homes in Abilene, Texas, and joined a small group of Christians who were interested in adopting. Slowly, Kim warmed up to the idea. However, as month after month passed, and they were still on the waiting list, Kim wondered again and again why God was not opening this door. Their faith was tested even more when every other couple in their group was chosen as adoptive parents.

Just when they were becoming despondent, a friend informed them of an opportunity for a private adoption through a family of an unwed teenage girl. Instead of trusting that God, who had led them to the Christian adoption agency in Texas was in control, they decided not to wait on Him.

"Even though I knew that God had led us to Christian Homes, I saw this new opportunity as my way of 'helping God out.' I was desperate for a baby and was going to solve this problem once and for all."

Without wasting time, Kim and her husband consulted a lawyer and concluded arrangements for adopting the baby as soon as he was born. Kim remembers the day the baby was born and the excitement that rippled through her body as they waited for the phone call from the lawyer representing them in the adoption process. The nursery in her home had been prepared and baby clothes were all laid out as the long period of their childlessness came close to an end.

As the lawyer left for the drive to the hospital to pick up the baby, Kim could barely contain the joy in her heart. God was finally answering her prayers. It wasn't the way she would have wanted Him to, but He was answering her positively. She was becoming a mother, and that thought alone gave her a deep sense of fulfillment.

As she waited for feedback that the baby had been picked up, the phone rang, and Kim ran to pick it up with a smile on her face. Her smile quickly faded, as she heard her lawyer's voice on the other line saying, "I am so sorry, Kim, but the mother has changed her mind. She wants to keep the baby."

Kim's world came crumbling down around her as she slowly handed the phone to her husband and went to her bedroom. Nothing made sense anymore, and Kim cried as if she would never stop. She recalls being an emotional wreck and not being able to function for the next few hours.

Unknown to Kim, she was about to reach a turning point that would forever change her life and her mindset.

"It was a Sunday morning. My husband went on to church, but I just could not stop crying. As I lay on the bed sobbing my heart out, it suddenly came to me: my desire to have a baby had become more important to me than God. This moment became my defining moment. It became clear that my infertility had consumed me, and I was on the brink of losing my soul. I remember sitting up in bed and resolving that nothing in life was that important. It took eight years of marriage and eight years of infertility to bring me to a point where I could confess that God was more important to me than anything else, and that He was all I needed." That moment changed Kim's life forever. She got up, washed her face, and when her husband came home from church, he was surprised by the transformation in his wife. The obsession with having a baby was gone completely.

SECTION REVIEW

3. The desire for something good easily consumes us and becomes an idol. For Kim, it was the desire for a child. What good desire(s) seem to be presently dominating your mind and thoughts and in what ways have you made these desires your idols?

_____

_____

_____

4. By asking Abraham to father a child by Hagar, Sarah was attempting to "help God" fulfill the promises He had made to Abraham. Kim admits to "helping God out" by seeking an alternative to the Christian adoption agency. Think back to situations in which you have tried "to assist" God. What has been the outcome of such situations? In what way does that outcome compare with Sarah and Kim's outcomes when they attempted to take matters into their own hands?

_____

_____

_____

Life returned to normal as Kim now sought a new purpose for her life. Barely a week later, they received a phone call from Christian Homes to pick up their adopted child. They were both surprised and pleased. God had to bring Kim to a point where she had no choice but to admit that she needed nothing else besides Him. It is when we arrive at that point, where we open wide our arms to embrace Him and Him only, that He fills us to overflowing with our heart's desires.

Kim's longing and desire for motherhood was finally realized as she and her husband brought home their baby girl in April 1987. Kim recalls bonding with the baby right from the beginning. She remembers the sense of fulfillment and peace that would often overcome her. Her most tender memories are of sitting on the porch in the evenings, rocking her baby, and praying over her. She would sing and pray, holding the answer to her prayers close and thanking God. Little did she know just how much those prayers would be needed in the years to come.

SECTION REVIEW

5. Often as parents, we wait until our children get into desperate situations to pray. Write down specific prayers that you can pray for your children in the following stages of life: (use additional paper, if necessary).

a. pre-natal...

b. birth and infancy ....

c. pre-school..

d. elementary ages ....

e. high school..

f. college...

g. adulthood ....

6. Write a personal prayer for your child in his /her present life-stage.

....

....

....

....

Some of the lessons that Kim learned through those years of crying out to the Lord include:

a. Christians must have a deep knowledge that God answers prayers and that in many situations prayer is one's only option. Such knowledge goes far beyond a belief in God and what He can do, for knowledge does not depend on how we feel or even on present circumstances. The Bible is full of injunctions to pray. (Jeremiah 33:2-3; John 14:13-14, 15:7; Philippians 4:6; Colossians 4:2; 1 Thessalonians 5:16-18;

James 5:13-16). It is also full of assurances that God answers prayers (2 Chronicles 7:14-15; Psalm 50:15, 65:1-2; Proverbs 15:29; Matthew 7:7-11; John 14:13-14; 1 John 5:14-15). The fact that He does not answer when we would want Him to or in the way we would like Him to should serve to build our faith, create trust, and remind us that "His ways are not our ways" (Isaiah 55:8). Surely the promise in Jeremiah 29:11 remains: "I know the thoughts that I think toward you, saith the Lord, thoughts of peace, and not of evil, to give you an expected end"(KJV).

b. Christians must constantly be aware that they do not have as much control as they think they do. It is easy to feel that if a person does the right things, he or she will get the right results. Therefore, it becomes difficult when one does all the right things, but gets unexpected results. It is at those times that we must trust God the most. Like the Apostle Paul, we often ask God to remove the thorn in our flesh. But what He tells us over and over is *My grace is sufficient for you* (2 Corinthians 12:9). All we can do in those times is trust.

c. Unmet expectations are meant to draw us closer to the Lord instead of away from Him. It is easy to trust God when He answers our prayers the way we want Him to, but trust, properly so called demands that we trust Him in the middle of the storm and when there is no light at the end of the tunnel.

d. There is a divine purpose for everything we are going through. God does not require that we praise Him only when things are the way we think they should be. He is deserving of our praise just because He is God. Every situation we face only serves to refine us and shape us into who He wants us to be. Kim stated that through everything she and her family have gone through, her favorite passage of scripture has been Habakkuk 3:17-18 which says:

Though the fig tree may not blossom,
Nor fruit be on the vines;
Though the labor of the olive may fail,
And the fields yield no food;
Though the flock may be cut off from the fold,

And there be no herd in the stalls—
Yet I will rejoice in the LORD,
I will joy in the God of my salvation. (NKJV)

If in spite of our struggles, through the heartaches, the tears, the grief, and the sleepless nights, we can say this, then God will be glorified, and it will all be well!

CHAPTER 3

When a Child Breaks Your Heart
(Train Up a Child in the Way He Should Go)

Youth fades; love droops;
The leaves of friendship fall:
A mother's secret hope outlives them all.
—Oliver Wendell Holmes

THE HEARTACHE KIM felt from the pain of wanting a child and not being able to have one, was lessened when God blessed them with their baby girl, adopted through Christian Homes. Kim had learned powerful life lessons from those years of waiting on the Lord, one of them being that nothing would ever separate her from the love of God. Her baby brought her joy, but she knew in the depths of her heart that whether she had a baby or not, God was the most important person in her life.

Often when God blesses, He keeps on blessing. Kim was pleased with the outcome from Christian Homes and was convinced that this was God's answer to their childlessness. In 1989, they asked to be placed on the agency's waiting list again. Nine months later, they brought home a baby boy.

Raising two kids was a delight for Kim, but she wasn't fully satisfied. In the deep recesses of her mind, she had always wanted at least three children. Because of the deep emotions and financial demands associated with adoption, Kim and her husband decided that another adoption was not an option. Although she fully supported her husband in this decision, Kim could not suppress the desire in her heart of wanting another baby, and she prayed about it constantly. She loved her adopted children deeply, but sometimes she would feel a sense of loss at not experiencing a baby growing inside of her. She refused to accept infertility as God's plan for her life and used the example that Jesus gave of the persistent widow as the basis for her prayers.

In 1991, Kim's persistent faith was rewarded when she got pregnant, just a year after her son's adoption, and her happiness knew no bounds. It was apparent to her that the God who knew her deepest desires was finally granting them. Kim believed that this was the response of a faithful God to her full surrender that Sunday morning in 1987.

Although it was a difficult pregnancy that kept her doctors concerned, Kim knew this was God's surprise gift and held on to the belief that this baby would be born safe and healthy. On April 29, 1992, Kim gave birth to a beautiful baby girl and finally felt as if her family was complete. She experienced God's promise that He would make her "a joyful mother of children" (Ps. 113:9) and settled comfortably into the role of wife and mother.

Raising three children under five years of age was quite demanding, but Kim was prepared for those demands physically, emotionally, and spiritually. The childhood years went by very quickly. Kim and her husband were as involved in the church as they had always been and did not miss any opportunity to engage their children in spiritual activities within and outside the church.

Like all kids, her children were growing up way too fast! Kim enjoyed those years, but it wasn't too long before she began noticing patterns of rebellion and withdrawal in her first daughter. Kim associated these attitudes with her daughter's feelings about being adopted. Kim and her husband believed in keeping communication lines open and would encourage their daughter to talk to them about her feelings. They intentionally created time and opportunity for both private and family discussions.

Despite their daughter's insistence that all was well, her attitude only got worse as she approached adolescence. The girl was eventually diagnosed with polycystic ovarian disease, and this seemed to partially explain her mood swings and emotional distress. In what was fast becoming her rebellious nature, she refused to take the prescribed medications and often reacted in anger which appeared to be directed particularly at Kim.

By the time their daughter was in high school, she was on an emotional rollercoaster. This period coincided with the time in which objects started disappearing from their home. Although her husband expressed suspicions about their daughter, Kim rejected such suspicions and believed it was important that they trust her implicitly.

When their daughter started dating, Kim and her husband expressed concerns about her choice of friend, but these concerns fell on deaf ears. Not long after that, they suspected that their daughter was drinking alcohol, although they never caught her drunk. The suspicion was strong enough that they confronted her often. Such confrontations always resulted in yelling matches which quickly took a toll on all the members of the family.

Kim felt the way they handled the initial stages of their daughter's problem was colored by their expectations. "My husband and I had been good kids. We pretty much did what we were told and had raised our kids to be the same way. We did not know how to handle our daughter's constant lies and deception." Eventually, they took her to Christian counselors and a Christian psychiatrist who diagnosed her with clinical depression and placed her on medication which again, she refused to take.

By the time their daughter was ready for college, they had confirmed she was an alcoholic, and this was difficult both to understand and to deal with. They confronted her often (despite her denials) and decided against sending her out of town to college. They insisted that she go to a local college so she could live at home for supervision and monitoring. The close monitoring placed a tremendous strain on their marriage as they each had different strategies for dealing with the problem. They would often blame each other for the person their daughter was becoming. Kim admits, "I couldn't come to terms with the fact that the child we waited so long for and prayed for so desperately was living a life so contrary to a life of seeking and serving God."

The situation continued to deteriorate. "The stress of finding filthy music in her car, catching her on the Internet corresponding with dubious guys we didn't know, and dating awful guys, finally reached a point where we wanted her out of the house so that we could raise the other two children in a peaceful, godly environment."

In her sophomore year, Kim and her husband finally allowed their daughter to move out of the house. She moved into the dorm at the local university, but three months later, she dropped out of college. By this time, they knew she was smoking and had confirmed that she was also using drugs. "We knew deep in our hearts that until she hit rock bottom, there was nothing that could be done to help her."

They could barely contain the pain and despair they felt as their daughter became a stranger in the grip of alcohol and drugs. They recalled a scene that took place after their daughter had dropped out of college and decided to rent a house with a friend of whom they strongly disapproved. Kim's husband went by to check on her one day, and the realization of the drug-infested pit she was living in hit him.

"This was our baby, one we had desperately prayed for, before and after we got her. We had done everything we knew to bring her and her siblings up in a God-fearing manner. In their childhood years they were always at church, involved in Bible school and Vacation Bible School, and yet there were other Christian parents who did not appear to be as diligent in raising their children as we were, and their kids were not into drugs and alcohol. This was hard for us to handle."

As their daughter slipped deeper into a lifestyle of drugs and alcohol, the strain on their marriage was becoming unbearable. They started blaming each other's parenting style. They slipped into self-doubt and began questioning God.

The source of their daughter's problem appeared rooted in her feelings of rejection by her birth mother, feelings that she kept denying until one day at her lowest point, she finally admitted it to Kim.

"She called me up and asked me to meet her for lunch. Once there, I asked her to tell me what was really going on and how we could help her. I'll never forget the look on her face when she said, 'You want to know how I really feel? I wish I was dead. I might as well be dead to her. I'll never understand how a mother can give up her little baby.'" Kim said that the minute her daughter voiced those sentiments, she knew there was a chance they would get their little girl back. "For the first time, my daughter was verbalizing emotions and feelings she had kept pent up for twenty years."

Soon after this, their daughter moved back into the house and Kim thought that by showering her with unconditional love and acceptance, things would quickly return to normal. But instead of things getting better, they got worse. Things started to go missing from their house again as their daughter began stealing to support her drug and alcohol addiction. They spent a lot of money getting psychiatric help for her as she went from one counselor to another. It appeared that nothing was working.

Finally, the hard decision was made to tell her to move out again. Kim wrote a letter to their daughter stating how much they loved her, but that they could no longer do anything to help her until she was ready to help herself. This was the hardest thing for Kim and her husband to do.

"Keeping her at home, at least we knew she was alive. But in our hearts, we knew that shielding her was not the right thing to do. We told her we loved her unconditionally, but there were boundaries in our home and she was breaking every one of them. We told her over and over that we would continue to cover her in our prayers."

Looking back, Kim feels that the offer and expression of unconditional love, albeit tough love, was important in helping their daughter make a change in her lifestyle. Their desire was that she would come to realize that as parents, they would always be there for her, loving her, and praying daily for her even though they would not support her lifestyle, and that she would always have a safe place to come back to.

Excited about her "freedom," their daughter moved to a bad part of town and began hanging out with a group of drug addicts. Kim and her husband felt powerless to help their child. All they could rely on was God's power to change her. In addition to their daily family and private prayers for their daughter, Kim depended heavily on the prayers of the ladies in her Bible study group. Kim admits that they went through a season of praying unceasingly for their daughter. "There were times I would just lay flat on the floor and pray till daybreak. Sometimes our only prayer would be, 'God please keep her alive just one more day, and maybe she'll come around.'" The thought in Scripture that kept them going was a passage in which Moses tells the rebellious Israelites, "I have never stopped praying for you." Their only hope was persistent prayer.

Amazingly, in spite of how bleak the situation looked, Kim admits knowing deep in her heart that their daughter would change. She says, "I knew how I prayed for her even before she was born and I knew what I prayed for her as I held her in my arms as a newborn baby. I kept remembering all those months I would sit on that swing and sing to her and pray for her. I remembered what I used to ask God for concerning my daughter. I knew without a doubt that God did not give her to us for her to lose her soul. That was what kept me going daily."

As the situation worsened, Kim recalls that she and her husband would pray desperate prayers. They often felt as if they were giving God a blank check and had no idea how He would use it, especially when they said prayers like, "Lord, do whatever you have to do to cause her to change." They trusted God to save their daughter.

Although there was no immediate dramatic change in their daughter's life during those days of intense prayer, Kim and her husband could tell their prayers were working. Kim recalls her daughter screaming into the phone one day, "Stop praying for me!" but instead of deterring them, that phrase gave them hope.

SECTION REVIEW

1. When have you had to show tough love to your children? How did they react? What was the final result of that tough love?

_____

_____

_____

2. The following passages of scripture encourage us to show tough love to our children: Proverbs 13:24; 20:18; 22:15; 23:13-14 (Note that these passages may not literally refer to physical spankings, but to any tough form of correction.) Read each of these passages and write down how their meanings can be practically applied in your efforts to raise godly children in an ungodly world.

_____

_____

_____

Although it took five months of ceaseless prayers and months that seemed more like years, matters eventually came to a head in September 2008. Kim's prayer /Bible study group decided to devote a week to pray for each other's children and to end that week with a fasting session for Kim's daughter. Looking back, Kim said, "I know that was what finally did it. As part of our prayers in my ladies group, we asked God for a sign. I remember asking God to do something dramatic—not subtle—but something dramatic that would bring our daughter home and within a few days, He did it in a surprising manner."

The Monday after the prayer/fasting session, Kim went to work and a colleague who was interested in their daughter's situation mentioned a Christian drug rehabilitation center that was doing wonders for her own daughter who was on drugs. She gave Kim the flyer, and after researching the facility, Kim knew it would be a good fit for their daughter. The only problem was getting their daughter to agree to go. Amazingly, God arranged the whole situation in a way that Kim could not have foreseen.

On the same day that Kim received the flyer about the rehabilitation center, their daughter was sober enough to go online and attempt completing a job application. As she opened her Myspace account she saw a note that read, "If your name is [Kim's daughter's name] and you were born on [Kim's daughter's birthday] and adopted by a youth minister and his wife who were living in Tennessee at the time, I am your birth mother, and I want you to know that I have prayed for you every day for the past twenty-one years."

The note had a great impact on their daughter who, for the first time, felt that she had not been rejected by her birth mother after all. Since everything she had been doing was a direct result of her feelings of rejection and abandonment, she was ready to change her life, but did not know how. Kim and her husband, noticing her desire for change, used the opportunity to remind her that there are no coincidences in the spiritual world. They told her that receiving her birth mother's note the same day Kim heard about the rehab center meant something. Kim felt that this was the dramatic sign they had asked God for and for the first time in years, their daughter listened. About a week later, the family drove to the treatment center in Georgia, where their daughter began the process of rehabilitation, a process that lasted for nine months.

SECTION REVIEW

3. Sometimes we find ourselves in situations in which we can no longer pray. Mention a few of these situations that you have either faced or are currently facing.

---

4. Why is it hard to pray in those situations?

_____

_____

_____

5. What specific promises can you claim that can be of help in situations like the ones mentioned above?

_____

_____

_____

6. One of the insights from Kim's experiences is the need for us to pray for each other. Write down the names of three or four ladies that you can contact this week to pray together over the phone. Make contact with these women, pray together, and watch God work.

_____

_____

_____

More than six years later, Kim's daughter is sober and clean, to the glory of God. Her relationship with Kim and the rest of the family is as it should be: one of mutual respect and love. While still in rehab, Kim initiated a meeting between their daughter and her birth mother. Slowly, through the years, they have gotten to know each other. Kim's daughter has grown into a delightful young lady, one who loves the Lord and has a great relationship with her parents and her siblings. Her life is a true testimony to the injunction that if we train up a child in the way he should go, through the twists and turns of life and despite the wrong choices they often make, there is always hope that they will return to the One who loves them above all.

In the past year, God has brought a wonderful young man into her life, one who loves her and loves the Lord. One of Kim's happiest days was the day that he asked her and her husband for their permission to propose to their daughter, and today the whole family is happily planning a wedding.

Although this story has a happy ending, Kim and her husband's faith has been greatly tested through the years. Kim feels strongly that some of the lessons she learned during the years of her daughter's struggle with drugs were lessons she could not have learned any other way. Those lessons include:

a. As we struggle through life, there is need to belong to a group of Christians who can come alongside each other and hold each other up in prayers. Life was not meant to be lived in isolation, hence the institution of the Church as a family of believers. Kim stressed the fact that she depended on other people's prayers at the most difficult times of her struggles. She traces the turning point in her daughter's life to the week of prayer and fasting by her ladies prayer group. Something will always be going on either in our lives, in the lives of our husbands, our children, or other family members such that we will never run out of things to pray about. It is important that we be in prayer for others as they also keep us covered in prayers.

b. Realizing that we have an enemy who attempts to use every situation in our lives to draw us away from God, Kim admits that the devil was constantly placing doubts in her mind. During the years of infertility, there were doubts about God's love for her. And during the years of her daughter's struggles, there were doubts about her mothering abilities. The only way to counter the devil's lies is to replace them with the promises in God's Word. And the only way to know what God's promises are is to read and study His Word daily. One of the promises Kim constantly claimed and affirmed was the promise of God in 1 Corinthians 10:13 that He would never allow us to be tempted above what we are able to bear.

c. A recent poll by the Barna group and the Gallup organization revealed that although 59% of American Christians read their Bible on occasion and only 16% read their Bibles on a daily basis. Reasons for the lack of daily Bible reading could range from a lack of time (women appear busier today than they have ever been) to not knowing exactly where and what to read. We need to be mindful of the fact that the only way to counter the lies of the devil is to carve out daily periods of time to read God's Word and affirm His promises. There are great resources for daily devotionals in the appendix section of this book.

d. "We need to let go of our pride especially where our children are concerned." In this one sentence, Kim confesses what every mother feels but far too often would never admit. Raising our children to be the "perfect kids" has an element of pride associated with it, for when our children do not act the way we would want them to, we take it as a reflection of ourselves and feel a deep sense of failure. It is easy to hold onto Proverbs 6:22 as a crutch, claiming that it promises that our children must turn out right if we do all the right things, but this crutch does not always hold us up.

e. Kim says, "Our children have choices, and sometimes, despite how good a parenting job we have done, they make the wrong choices." If that happens, all we can do is trust that God, to whom our children belong in the first place, will use those awful choices as teaching and pruning tools to bring them back to Him. We also need to trust that the seeds we planted in their lives will eventually bring forth good fruit and that if we keep on praying unceasingly for them and loving them unconditionally, they will one day, like the prodigal son, come home. As hard as it is to deal with, God often uses our children to humble us.

SECTION REVIEW

7. Unmet expectations often pull us away from God, but for Kim, they drew her closer. What specific actions can be taken to help draw you close to God during times of adversity?

_____

_____

_____

8. Every child struggles with something at one point or another. For Kim's child it was drugs and alcohol. What is (are) your child(ren) currently struggling with?

_____

_____

_____

9. What practical steps can be taken by you and your child to deal with this situation?

_____

_____

_____

10. Kim's constant source of comfort was found in 1 Corinthians 10:13 and in Habakkuk 3:17-18. Read these passages and attempt committing them wholly or in part to memory. What other passages of scripture contain promises that you can claim for whatever you are going through right now?

_____

_____

_____

CHAPTER 4

An African Mother's Story
(Be Not Dismayed What E'er Betide)

Motherhood is a call to make sacrifices and I think a fulfilled mother is one who makes those sacrifices happily.
—Affiong Mkpong

IN THE SMALL African village of *Ntan Ekere,* a village nestled among the rolling hills of Southeastern Nigeria, a baby girl was born. The year was 1944, and virtually every African couple's desire at that time, was to have a baby boy as their first child, for sons grew up to be the heirs and future family heads while daughters were married off at an early age and were more useful to their marital families than to their birth families.

For Affiong, the newborn baby, life would be a little different. She would grow up to be the apple of her father's eye, and privileges which were almost exclusively reserved for sons, would be extended to and enjoyed by her. One such notable privilege was formal education. It was almost unheard of for girls to be sent to schools of learning in Nigeria in the 1940's, but Affiong was the exception to that rule. Her father, noticing her bright and inquisitive mind even at an early age, went against tradition and enrolled her in the nearby primary school when she was six years old.

Affiong learned at an early age to stand up for herself, to expect the best of herself, and to always give her utmost effort to whatever was expected of her. Despite being the only girl in a class of boys, she excelled. She quickly rose to the top of her class, became fluent in the English language, and finished primary school in 1956. Although her desire was to continue going to school, she was the first of fifteen children, and family responsibilities and financial constraints resulted in her working immediately after primary school.

In 1960, Affiong was employed as a teacher's aide by the African Christian Schools Foundation to work in one of the newly-established Christian primary schools. This employment meant her leaving home at a young age, but Affiong was ready. Her position as the first daughter in a large family had prepared her for life. She was independent, hardworking, and focused. It was rare for young ladies to live on their own in those days, but her parents confidently sent her out into the world with two younger siblings to accompany her.

At the age of sixteen, Affiong became the head of a household of three. Her reputation as a serious-minded teacher's aide won her the love and admiration of her students and co-workers. Her life at that time revolved around her classroom, her siblings, and her gardens. Like most African children at the time, she grew up working on her parent's farms and had earlier developed a love for farming. She cultivated almost every spare piece of land in the school premises and spent every spare moment in her gardens. She admits, "I loved planting, preparing the soil, planting seeds, and then watching them sprout and grow gave me a deep sense of satisfaction. I loved harvesting vegetables from my gardens and making meals using my own produce instead of wasting money buying things in the market that I could grow. Working in the farms gave me time to think and kept me from distractions." This love for farming would grow in the years to come and would be of great advantage to Affiong.

While teaching at Christian Primary School, Afaha Effiat, in 1963, Affiong met the man that would become her husband. At first, it appeared they were as different as night and day. He was strong-willed and outgoing with a belief that women had their place, while Affiong was forthright with strong opinions, believing that women had the same right as men to achieve all that life had to offer. This and other differences created initial tension between them, but the closer they worked together, the more they began to respect each other. His mother, during one of her visits to the school, met and fell in love with the industrious Affiong and took advantage of every opportunity to bring the two young people together. The better Affiong got to know this young man, the more she liked him. It didn't take long for them to fall in love and become engaged.

Marriage followed soon after to the great delight of his mom and of all who knew this couple. Married life was all that Affiong had hoped it would be. She had a husband who loved her and a mother-in-law, who had always wanted, but never had a daughter, who treated her like the daughter she always wanted but never had. Life was soon to play a cruel joke on Affiong that would change her life forever. Only a week after their wedding in 1964, her mother-in-law who was paying them a surprise visit, had a stroke and died in Affiong's arms. Affiong's first struggle began. Her security in marriage, apart from the love of her husband, was the bond between her and her mother-in-law.

Affiong knew that her husband's uncles, their wives, and their children neither liked nor accepted her. She had three strikes against her. First, because she was from a different part of the state, she was viewed as someone from a different tribe and thus discriminated against. Second, as an educated female, she was shunned by the other females in the extended family. Third, she was a partner in a love marriage, not an arranged marriage, as was the custom at the time.

All she wanted to do when her mother-in-law, *Mamma,* died was go back home to the love and security of her birth family, but she knew she couldn't. Drawing on the strength gained from her past experiences of surviving against all odds, Affiong knew she had to gain the respect of her husband's family by being herself and showering them with love.

She moved into the family house in the village during school holidays and decided to impact the family by hard work and determination. Since the predominant duties of women at that time centered on farming, Affiong's desire to be accepted by her in-laws and her love for gardening led her to begin farming in earnest. She spent every minute outside of the classroom working in her backyard garden, which later grew into produce farms all over the school premises. She started growing subsistent and economic crops in her husband's village and this soon gained her the nickname of *"mma inwang"* (literally translated as "farm lady").

Affiong missed *Mamma* very much, and her role included being the sole source of consolation to her husband who, being an only child, desperately missed the close relationship between him and his mother. In October of the same year, another source of consolation came in the form of their newborn baby which they named Idongesit (literally translated as "My Comforter"). Affiong often said that she and her husband took one look at that baby and have never mourned the loss of *Mamma* again.

Affiong's child-bearing years progressed rapidly with five children being born between 1964 and 1973 and then her "surprise baby" coming two decades later in 1987. Although she had hoped that having children would lessen the constant criticisms from her husband's extended family, Affiong's only way of proving herself a worthy wife was by enduring their critical attitudes and raising her children in the fear and admonition of the Lord. She recalled that the loneliness she felt at those times, with her husband being her only friend in a large extended family, made her more sensitive to others and drew her into an intimate relationship with God. "God became my friend and confidante. I would spend many hours reading my Bible or talking to Him or singing about Him to my little children. I began teaching my children to memorize portions of scripture both in English and in Efik (the native language), and my children became my friends, a bond which only grew stronger as they grew older."

SECTION REVIEW

1. In the book, *What Do You Want from Me?*, Terri Apter, a psychologist at Cambridge University, uses research gathered over the past twenty years to show that the relationship between female in-laws can be very intense. Apter discovered that more than 60% of women feel that friction with their in-laws is a recurrent source of stress. What are some of the causes of stress in your in-law relationships?

_____

_____

_____

2. What practical things can be done to minimize the stress in in-law relationships as we seek to "live peaceably with all men?" (Romans 12:18 NKJV)

_____

_____

_____

3. Mention two *specific* ways that you will reach out to your mother-in-law or sister-in-law(s) this week.

_____

_____

_____

Two years after marriage, Affiong's husband was given the opportunity of preaching the Gospel in a small congregation three miles from where they lived. And so Affiong took on the role of a preacher's wife at the young age of nineteen. The challenges of this new role in addition to her duties as an elementary school teacher, a wife, and a mother, were easily handled by Affiong who had a love for people. She was at her best when speaking at ladies' Gospel meetings or giving advice to other preachers' wives. Just when she was getting adept at balancing these roles, her husband was admitted to a university in the United States for further training as a Gospel preacher. Although this was a great opportunity for him, it meant that their family would be divided.

Even though the initial plan was for Affiong and her husband to travel to America together, Affiong could not imagine leaving her children behind. Her own parents and other family members were ready to care for the children while she was away, but Affiong did not think anybody could raise her children the way she wanted them raised.

"My children were my first mission field; I had a responsibility to raise them for the Lord. Since the early years were the most important learning times in a child's life and my children ranged from eight months to six years, I just could not leave them behind." Affiong made the painful decision to stay behind in Nigeria and raise her children while her husband left for America.

Those months of separation were extremely hard, especially since her husband had been her best friend for so long. Being both mother and father to her children was not an easy task. Her husband was a strict disciplinarian, and so Affiong had to step in and fill those shoes. She began by setting specific family expectations and was quick to follow through with consequences. Daily family devotionals, which were initiated by her husband early on in the marriage, continued. She initiated evening devotions as a time to teach her children to memorize Bible passages. Some of her children's greatest childhood memories center on sitting on the floor after supper with their mother as she used the light from a kerosene lantern to teach them the Psalms in their native language.

SECTION REVIEW

4. With an increase in military families and other job related separations, mothers are often left to raise children alone for long periods of time. Affiong used this time to ensure that traditions started by her husband were maintained and that her children were grounded in the Word of God. Make a list of five things that a mother can do during times of separation (or in any other situation where she is forced by circumstances to be the spiritual leader of her home) to ensure the spiritual growth and development of the children.

---

5. Moments of separation can also affect the closeness of our relationship with our husbands. What are some specific things that can be done to maintain intimacy between husbands and wives despite distance?

Although she never regretted her decision, and took comfort in seeing her children blossom under her love and care, Affiong lived for the letters that came every two months from America. She prayed that God would make the years of her husband's studies go by very fast so that her family would be together again. Affiong's prayers were answered, but in a different way than she had thought. Ten months after her husband left, she received a letter from him stating that the congregation that he worshipped with in Henderson, Tennessee, seeing how much he missed his family, had made financial arrangements for his family to join him in the United States. Affiong and the children were overjoyed.

"Although it was hard leaving my parents, siblings, and other family members behind, I knew I needed to be with my husband. The children needed to be raised by both parents. Also, the opportunity of exposing them to life in another culture was one that we could not pass up."

In January 1972, precisely a year after her husband had traveled to America, Affiong and the children left Nigeria and arrived in the United States. The children were quickly placed in schools, and Affiong's quick mind and her love for learning led to her admission into Watkins Institute in Nashville, Tennessee, where she studied and received a diploma in Home Economics.

In 1973, her husband completed a Masters Degree program, and it was time for the family to make a serious decision about their future. Her husband had the opportunity of settling down in America and raising his family in what was undoubtedly a more advanced society, but he felt a strong responsibility to his home country of Nigeria. The church in Nigeria was fledgling at best, and he could provide the leadership and the impetus for growth. His Master's degree in Educational Administration and Supervision would be useful in a developing country that had attained independence thirteen years earlier and needed all available manpower. He was an only child, and the society expected him to build on the heritage left behind by his father (something he could not do if he were 8,000 miles away in another country).

Finally, it was important to him that the children be raised as Nigerians, something that could more easily be done if they were raised in Nigeria. These were the thoughts and issues that dominated their minds during the sleepless nights before his graduation from Middle Tennessee State University and finally led to the decision to return to Nigeria. Affiong encouraged her husband in his decision to move back to Nigeria.

"It would have been easy to stay in America, but I knew we belonged in Nigeria. Surely life would be harder there both for us and for the children (who had become used to living in an American society). We had to look beyond the present into the many ways that God would use us to make a difference for our people back home. Too many people settle for the better life in America, but how can their own countries be better unless those who have seen the better life take that life back home and make a difference? I did not want my children to simply enjoy a better life, I wanted them to grow up and make a difference. Therefore, we went back to Nigeria where we belonged."

Before leaving the United States, her husband had made contact with people who were interested in visiting Nigeria, and his plan was to establish relationships between those people and Christians back in Nigeria. Although his oldest child was only ten years old, he also made arrangements for her and her siblings to one day return to America for their college education. And so it was that one by one, all of Affiong's six children eventually returned to Freed-Hardeman College, his alma mater.

Settling back into a Nigerian lifestyle was fairly easy for Affiong and her family. Her husband initially worked as a high school teacher, and was subsequently promoted to the position of principal. Affiong, having received a certificate as a trained teacher, started teaching in an elementary school. The best part about teaching at that level was that she became her children's first teacher. During those child-rearing years, Affiong was very industrious. She modeled for her children the virtues seen in the woman of Proverbs 31, getting up early to make pancakes, puff-puff, bean cakes, and other food items to sell to the children in the nearby schools who often came to school without breakfast.

In order for her children to thrive in the Nigerian economy, Affiong knew that neither she nor her husband could depend only on their monthly paychecks. Therefore she became a major distributor for soft drink companies like Dr. Pepper and Coca Cola. She also supplemented the family's food budget by growing vegetables and staples on a large scale. Many of the memories of her children's early years centered around processing the cassava harvested from their farm into *garri*, the staple of the Nigerian diet. One grown child recollects:

While growing up, we knew our parents could afford to buy anything we needed, but mummy taught us the joys of working hard and growing our own food. We spent afternoons working together in one farmland or another as a family, planting, harvesting, or weeding. We spent evenings processing the things we harvested, peeling cassava, grating it into *foofoo,* or sifting and frying *garri.* Mum was always there using every opportunity to teach us, correct us, or instill values into our lives. Although being a teacher placed her in the upper middle class of our society, she never allowed us to take advantage of that fact nor of the fact that we had grown up in the United States.

Her husband's reputation as a hardworking principal meant that he was often transferred from one ailing school to another. But Affiong made the various moves an adventure for her children. One by one, her children finished high school and left home to study in the United States. Leaving home was extremely hard for these children for whom home had been a place of love and refuge, but Affiong always made their leaving exciting. She never let them forget that obtaining a Christian education was a privilege from God Himself and one they could not take lightly.

Each child recalls almost identically, the rituals associated with leaving home. The day would begin with morning devotions, like every other day, but with special prayers for the departing child in which the family would invariably sing, "Be not dismayed whate'er betide, God will take care of you," with Affiong singing loudly enough to drown out the other voices. This special prayer session was followed by a special breakfast to which uncles, aunties, grandparents, and cousins were invited.

Everybody had a word of advice for the departing child. The long drive to the airport was always filled with anecdotes about the family, last minute advice, and a reminder of the family's expectations. Then with one last hug, Affiong would send her child off with a promise to be there when they returned, a promise she kept for five of her six children.

Although the days of releasing her children to study 8,000 miles away from home were difficult days, Affiong had no regrets. She believed firmly that:

> It is easy to let go of something that is not really yours. Those children were not mine to begin with; I was just a caretaker for a little while. Realizing that the only way they could have a Christian education at that time was to go back to America, I placed them in the hands of their Heavenly Father and prayed that the foundation we had laid during their childhood would be solid enough to ensure their growing up to be useful vessels in His Kingdom. Of course I missed them terribly. My children and I were very close, but my prayer had always been that my children would make a difference in their generation and to do that, they would need the very best education. A day did not go by that I did not miss them—there was a constant ache in my heart for them—but neither did a day go by that I did not pray for them individually and I knew in my heart that they were okay. That was good enough for me.

SECTION REVIEW

6. Affiong felt strongly that she wanted her children to grow up and make a difference in their own society. In America today, people all around us have needs. What are specific ways that you can teach and encourage your children to meet these needs and make a difference in the world around them?

_____

_____

_____

7. It was important to Affiong that her children do things together to build a strong bond as a family. Families today are often going in separate directions with every one doing their own thing.

What changes need to be made in your family to ensure that every member grows together instead of apart?

_____

_____

_____

8. Affiong's mindset, where her children were concerned, was that "It is easy to let go of something that is not really yours. Those children were not mine to begin with; I was just a caretaker for a little while." What specific things would you change in the way you raise your children, if you adopted this mindset?

_____

_____

_____

Affiong felt strongly that the greatest sacrifice she had to make as a mother was releasing her children to study so far from home, but according to her, "motherhood is full of sacrifices and I think a fulfilled mother is one who makes those sacrifices happily. Having said that though, the happiest days of my life were the days my children returned to Nigeria with their degrees."

Affiong's life was marked by a series of transitions. One transition happened in 1985 when her husband retired early from his job as a school principal and followed the call to start a School of Preaching in what was then known as Cross River State. Although she continued teaching in a nearby elementary school, she began investing her time and energy in the newly established school. Since her husband brought the same determination and drive that he had exhibited as a public school principal to the School of Preaching, the school grew rapidly. In a period of three years the school grew into the Nigerian Christian Institute (NCI) embodying a full-fledged boarding high school, the only Christian high school in the state at that time, and a school of preaching.

When Affiong retired from the State Service in 1996, she immediately stepped into the role of a matron at the NCI. As matron, her duties included the supervision of the dormitories, the purchasing of food items for the cafeteria, supervising the cafeteria and boarding house staff, dealing with disciplinary problems involving female students, and simply being a mother to the over nine hundred high school students who lived away from home and needed a mother's love. Being known as the mother of NCI brought a special joy to Affiong's heart and gave her a purpose, especially since her own children were getting married and having families of their own.

Another period of transition in Affiong's life was in 1990 when her husband was invited to contest elections for the mayoral seat of Uyo local government in the southeastern region of Nigeria. At that time, the debate about whether Christians should be involved in politics was an ongoing one in Nigeria, and she wasn't sure if her husband should blaze that trail. In their characteristic way, they decided to fast and pray for guidance on making the right decision. The desire to place the needs of the people of Uyo above personal considerations led them to the decision that he should contest.

Affiong remembered the days leading to and immediately following the elections. "I do not remember when I prayed more for my husband. Nigerian politics at that time was a dirty game, full of corrupt politicians who knew how to play the game. My husband was a preacher and a Christian school proprietor. He knew nothing about politics except that he loved his people and wanted the best for them. My prayers were that he would only win the election if it was God's will to use Him mightily in politics to make a difference."

To the surprise of the seasoned politicians who contested for the post, her husband won the election and was sworn into office on January 30, 1991. Affiong's journey as the First Lady of Uyo local government began. Since Uyo was the capital of the newly created Akwa Ibom State, there were many demands on the First Lady (affectionately called Mma Uyo) whose mandate was to make life better for the rural woman. Affiong spent many hours in meetings with the governor's wife and her cabinet planning strategies and campaigns. She was given an official vehicle and a chauffeur to drive her to the ninety villages which make up the Local Government Council Area. Like she did everything else, Affiong approached this new assignment with determination and zeal. She arranged briefing sessions with the women in the villages, assessing their needs and becoming their voice with the state administration.

Using her love for farming as a spring board, she encouraged the women to form co-operative societies and engage in commercial farming instead of the subsistence farming for which they were known. She organized the "Better Life for Rural Women Seminars" which discussed building successful marriages, managing family finances, operating home-based businesses, and parenting issues for the women in Uyo. She quickly became the most loved First Lady in the state. "I believed that my primary task was to show Christ to the least of the women in Uyo Local Government Council Area. I knew without a doubt that God placed me in that position for a reason, and I was determined to honor Him in everything I did. Politics became just one more tool to use in serving Him by serving others."

In December 1993, their first term as mayor and first lady was over. Despite pressure from the people of Uyo that they seek a second term, Affiong and her husband decided to give up politics and return to their school. They felt that in a small way they had changed the face of politics, proving that Christians could go into politics and use their position as a vehicle for change. Their brief excursion into politics was an opportunity that changed the city of Uyo forever, and Affiong gave God all the glory.

Their return to fulltime duties at NCI brought a period of rapid growth to the school. Their experiences as mayor and first lady were useful in the administration of the Institute. In just a few years the school's curriculum expanded to include Associate Degree Programs in Bible, Business Studies, and Mass Communication. Affiong and her husband were given various awards, not just for their services in politics but also for their contributions in the field of Christian education.

By this time, they had become grandparents, and life took on a slightly slower pace. Although she was still the matron of the NCI, Affiong settled well into her role as a grandmother. With two of her children residing in the United States with their husbands at that time, she began traveling internationally to visit them and enjoy her American grandchildren. At the birth of her eighteenth grandchild in 2009, Affiong felt that her life had come full circle. She had come a long way. From struggling to make ends meet as the young wife of a poor preacher in 1964, God had used her to raise a generation of God-fearing men and women, a generation into which she had instilled a love for the Lord and the virtues of hard work, determination to succeed, and sacrificial living.

When Affiong died peacefully in her sleep on March 30, 2010, nine days before her sixty-sixth birthday and the day after her forty-sixth wedding anniversary, it was agreed by the more than 5,000 people who attended her funeral that a worthy woman had gone on to her reward. Insight into her life would reveal the following life lessons:

a. The world stands by and makes way for persons who know where they are headed. From a young age, Affiong knew that the advantage of being educated meant that much was expected of her, and she expected much of herself. No matter how hard it was to succeed, she kept pushing forward. She did more for her family of birth than all her brothers combined by building, with her husband, the first concrete home for her parents and ensuring that her younger brothers and her own children reached the height of education that they desired to reach. One of her favorite sayings was, "I may not have a Ph.D but because my children have Ph.Ds, it means I too have a Ph.D."

b. A successful mother is one who is ready to make sacrifices happily for her children. From the time she refused to leave her children behind and travel with her husband to America, to the time she released them to go to school 8,000 miles away from home, Affiong was constantly sacrificing for her children. A tribute written by one of her daughters to honor her at the funeral read, "As we mourn your loss, we also celebrate the legacy you have given us. You have bequeathed to us the Spirit of loving our children and sacrificing as much as necessary to provide for them.… You have taught us by example how to be a Proverbs 31 woman."

c. Marriage is a life-time commitment. Affiong got married at age twenty and stayed married to the same husband for forty-six years. One of the pieces of advice she always gave young ladies was that marriage is not a commitment one makes to a man but rather a commitment made to God. Since the One we make the commitment to never changes, He does not expect us to change. One of the scriptures that she drilled into her four daughters was Proverbs 14:1, "A wise woman builds her own home" (NLT), believing that it is the woman in the home who determines the type of home her children grow up in, whether it is one of joy, laughter, and peace or one of strife, bitterness, and rivalry.

d. One can never be so rich that they do not "play with dirt." For Affiong, "playing with dirt" meant bending down and planting things in the soil, whether it was a garden or a pot. She did not believe there was greater joy than seeing seeds emerge from the soil and watching them grow. At the time of her death, Affiong had just finished planting cassava in four hectares of land, an equivalent of six acres. Science has caught up with her thoughts, and there is mounting evidence to support the therapeutic effects of planting. One such evidence is seen in an article by Mark Epstein in the *Seattle Daily Journal of Commerce* titled "The Garden as Healer." He writes:

> People relate to plants. That is the basis for therapeutic landscape design and horticultural therapy. Therapeutic gardens are designed for children, for those with temporary or permanent physical disabilities, for patients

with Alzheimer's disease, for the elderly, for those with terminal illnesses and their families, and for prison inmates. They are large and small, fully accessible or only for viewing, and for day and night use. They are as varied as our culture. Their value lies in the positive associations people have with plants. Plants have aesthetic, temporal and spiritual qualities. The annual dormancy and rejuvenation of plants mark time, and provides a sense of connection to the earth and to other living organisms. A garden can restore a sense of order, safety and privacy for those dealing with the chaos induced by illness. The act of gardening produces a peaceful, effortless concentration that increases our capacity to rest. It creates more outward perceptions rather than inward self-consciousness, a valuable balance to the uneasiness of illness. A therapeutic garden creates a complementarity between life and place. While the therapeutic value of the garden is being rediscovered, it has roots deep in time.

Affiong's philosophy of life is that life is meant to be lived to the full. Her advice is to "enjoy life; spend time doing the things that you want to do and make life an adventure." Many ladies expect to find fulfillment exclusively in their roles as wife and mother and become discouraged when those roles do not bring the satisfaction they crave. Although her children confess that Affiong was a great mother, her life was not wrapped up in her children. She allowed them the freedom that independence brings and found her fulfillment in doing the things she felt called by the Lord to do. Her passion included teaching at ladies gospel meetings all over the state, forming associations and co-operative societies, farming extensively, employing local farmers to work on her farmland, owning various shops in which she sold the produce from her farm, and traveling overseas whenever she wanted to. As ladies, we need to focus on being who God wants us to be as individuals. As mothers, we need to view motherhood as just one of many different roles in which we are to glorify God.

Section Review

9. Although Christian involvement in politics appears more acceptable today than in the early 1990's, the ratio of Christians to non-Christians in political offices is still low. Carry out an Internet search to find out how many Christians are in political offices in your state and county. What can Christians do to increase this number?

_____

_____

_____

10. Which of the life lessons gleaned from Affiong's life is most needed in your own life?

_____

_____

_____

11. What practical steps can be taken to help incorporate that lesson into your daily life?

_____

_____

_____

12. What accountability procedures will you put in place to ensure that those practical steps are taken?

_____

_____

_____

CHAPTER 5

Dealing With Infidelity and Betrayal in a Way That Honors God
(For I, the Lord, Know the Plans I Have for You)

Distance tests a horse's strength just as time reveals a person's character.

—Chinese proverb

MANY CHRISTIAN GIRLS dream of meeting a godly Christian man, falling in love, getting married and raising godly children. Gee felt as if she was living that dream as she stood at the altar beside her groom in 1960, just two days after graduating from high school. She had been led to the Lord by him, and the exciting life of an Air Force wife awaited her. Having lost her mom when she was only two-and-a-half years old, her prayer as she said her vows on that Sunday afternoon was that God would one day give her children and keep her alive to raise them.

Marriage took her only an hour-and-a-half away from her father, grandparents, and other family members who had so lovingly raised her since her mother's death. She quickly settled down into being a wife to this man whom she adored. God heard her prayers, and fourteen months later, she gave birth to her first child. In November 1963, she gave birth to another child, her daughter, and to another son in 1968. Being a mother brought her more joy than she had ever known, but it also increased her worries about being alive to raise her children. "I knew what it was like to grow up without a mother, and I did not want that for my children." Instead of allowing those fears to cripple her, Gee drew closer to God and implored Him daily to keep her alive to raise her children.

Section Review

1. Traumatic experiences often determine the things we are afraid of. Gee's fear of being alive to raise her children was a result of losing her mom as a toddler. What traumatic experiences have you gone through in your life?

_____

_____

_____

2. What fears have these experiences created?

_____

_____

_____

3. Instead of being crippled by her fears, Gee laid them at the feet of the only One who could do something about them. Read Philippians 3:6-7 and 1 Peter 5:7. Write a prayer telling God your deepest fears and handing them over to Him. (Use additional paper if you need to.)

_____

_____

_____

The migratory life of a service man's wife began for Gee in 1965 when her husband was stationed in Germany. A mother of two at the time, Gee and the children lived with her family and with his family for three months before joining him. Two years later, they moved again to England. Before his retirement from the Air Force, they had moved eight times.

Gee never considered staying behind in the United States while her husband moved from one assignment to another. She and the children went along on every move. "I believed strongly that my place was beside my husband and that the children and I added some stability to his life. It was important that the children be raised by both parents and so my duty was to make every move an adventure for them."

When her husband retired, he became restless, moving from Florida to Texas to attend a Bible School, deciding two years into the program that it wasn't what he wanted, and then moving the family again, back to Florida. During this time, Gee noticed that her husband was not only becoming restless, but that he was showing signs of a dual personality. He was harsh and verbally abusive at home, but would be attentive, gentle, and kind in public. She tried excusing his behavior and his moods by focusing on his positive characteristics. "He was such a generous provider for the children and me, never complaining about paying the bills or purchasing anything we needed, and I felt that it made up for all the times he treated us in a mean and vicious manner."

Gee often felt that something was wrong with her husband's behavior but did not know how to handle his frequent angry outbursts and verbal abuses or whom to talk to about them. When he would react in a harsh manner toward the children, becoming verbally and physically abusive, Gee would plead with him. But the pleas would fall on deaf ears as he would react in anger toward her, blaming her for not being strict enough in the way she raised the children. What confused the whole family was that at other times he would be a very supportive and loving husband. Gee and the children were always walking on egg shells, never knowing when his angry outbursts would erupt, especially since his anger easily erupted over seemingly nothing. Gee's husband had such a good reputation as a strong Christian man that she felt nobody would believe her even if she voiced her concerns.

"This was at a time when the Church felt that submissiveness as a wife meant being a doormat. If I had told anyone what we were going through, I probably would have been told that I should try harder to please him so that he would not get angry with me. It would have been my fault."

Section Review

4. The Bible teaches wives to be submissive to their husbands as unto the Lord (see Ephesians 5:22). How is it possible to obey this injunction in an abusive relationship?

_____

_____

_____

5. The National Coalition Against Domestic Violence is a nonprofit organization dedicated to working toward a peaceful society where domestic violence no longer exists. Visit their website at www.ncadv.org/files/DomesticViolenceFactSheet and make a list of resources available to women who are in abusive relationships.

_____

_____

_____

6. Plan a class, group, or an individual visit to a shelter for abused women and write a report of your visit. What practical things can be done as a class, group, or individual, as a result of your visit, to make a difference in the lives of these women?

_____

_____

_____

7. People who are abused tend to be in denial for a long time. Discuss some telltale signs that someone might be suffering from verbal, emotional, or physical abuse and write some of those signs below. Befriend someone from a shelter for abused women or anyone in the church or community that you suspect might be a victim of abuse.

_____

_____

_____

In 1981, Gee's husband decided that the only way to curb his restlessness was to become a truck driver. This job took him all over the country, and Gee noticed that he became a different person. He would be gone for two weeks at a time, calling her two or three times a day while on the road. This job appeared to calm him down a little and the years passed by as they raised their children and as they became deeply involved in their local congregation. Gee's husband became a great Bible teacher and eventually an elder in their congregation. He was well loved by all in the church and in the community. As they grew old together, Gee often felt that all of her prayers had been answered. Her children were settling into their own roles as parents, blessing them with grandchildren. It appeared that they had weathered the storms associated with marital life, and Gee was looking forward to her golden years married to her teenage sweetheart, the first and only love of her life.

In 2006, she began making retirement plans, which included finding a buyer for her tax business and retiring early so that she and her husband could travel and enjoy growing old together. These plans coincided with her forty-sixth wedding anniversary, and she planned to celebrate it in a big way, not knowing that the greater part of her marriage had been a farce, and that the events which were about to unfold would bring her more heartache than she ever could have imagined.

It was a beautiful May morning, and Gee had an appointment 30 minutes out of town, at the social security office. At her husband's encouragement, she decided to leave the house early to spend some time walking around the mall and enjoying some alone time before her mid-morning appointment. She had barely reached the end of her long driveway when she realized that she had forgotten some original documents needed for her appointment. Thankful that she had not gone too far, she turned the car around and went back home to get the documents. As she unlocked the door, she was immediately prompted by her spirit to enter the house quietly without announcing her arrival.

Looking back, Gee attributes this prompting to the suspicions that had been playing on the fringes of her mind for the past few months. Although she trusted her husband implicitly, often naively, she had become concerned about some of his behavior. His refusal to get caller identification or call waiting features on their land line, the fact that the phone was always busy when she called home, and the fact that he never had reasonable explanations about his whereabouts, had all raised suspicions in her mind. She often brushed these suspicions aside, but this day Gee listened to her spirit, entered the house quietly, and made her way to the bedroom where the documents were kept. Just outside the bedroom door she paused as she heard her husband talking on the phone and making plans to meet someone for ice-cream.

Innocently wondering if it was one of their grandchildren or other relatives, her heart skipped a beat as she heard her husband declaring his love to a lady who was a recent visitor to their congregation. Gee listened with tears streaming down her face, her world slowly falling apart. She cried faintly as he said his goodbyes so he could shower and meet the lady on the other side of the phone for their ice-cream date. As he rushed into the shower, she could no longer control her sobs and tears, and it was these tears that brought her husband rushing out of the bathroom to her side. Realizing she had overheard the whole conversation, he pleaded with her and became extremely distraught.

Gee was overcome with sorrow, but she resolved to forgive her husband who initially showed signs of remorse. She was willing to work on salvaging her marriage, but it was soon obvious that her husband was not ready to give up the adulterous relationship. He continued making calls to his mistress and would sneak off to meet her, despite Gee's pleas to both him and the lady he was involved with.

Two months later, Gee realized that she could no longer live in a farce of a marriage. "The hardest part of this was the children. Although they were grown, I knew they would be devastated. I was willing to work things out with my husband for their sake, for the sake of the Gospel, and because of the forty-six years we had spent together, but my husband was no longer interested in a monogamous marriage."

Gee and her husband were referred to a Christian counselor but her husband stopped going after the first few sessions. Four months after trying to work things out, Gee was encouraged by her children, family members, and church members to file for legal separation. To her dismay, her husband moved out of the home they had built together and lived in for twenty-five years, into the house of his mistress.

Those were awful days for Gee, and she spent many hours blaming herself; wondering what she could have done differently and how she could possibly have prevented this situation in her marriage. "I was as good a wife as I knew how to be. I treated my husband as lord and master, waiting on him hand and foot and granting his every wish and desire. I did not know what I could have done differently."

Gee's relationship with God was the only thing that kept her sane through those days. "My only source of comfort was the Word of God. I spent hours reading the Psalms and just letting His words soak into my heart and my soul." As she spent time in the Word, one of the passages of Scripture that resonated within her Spirit was Jeremiah 29:11, "'For I know the thoughts that I think toward you,' saith the LORD, 'thoughts of peace, and not of evil, to give you an expected end," (KJV). This became one of her favorite passages, and she committed it to memory, saying it over and over every day. "It gave me comfort just to know that in the middle of all I was going through, God was keeping me in His thoughts and would make everything alright."

Section Review

8. Gee found out about her husband's unfaithfulness by listening to her spirit. Often we feel the nudging of God in our spirit and the more we listen and obey, the stronger His voice becomes. What is the Spirit of God within you nudging you to do today?

\
\
\

9. Matthew 19:9 is one of the Bible passages often used to support adultery as a reason for divorce. Gee was willing to forgive her husband and keep her marriage together despite the betrayal. Why is it easier to divorce on "spiritual grounds" than to forgive? What are some situations in which forgiveness would be a better alternative?

\
\
\

10. Gee found comfort and solace in the Word of God. What are five Bible passages that can bring comfort in times of grief or loss? Share these passages and commit to memorizing one passage a week for the next five weeks, using them often when there is a need to feel God's presence.

\
\
\

When her husband moved out, Gee began the long process of trying to make sense out of everything that had happened. The emotional stress she was under affected her physically, and she was diagnosed with bleeding ulcers. Her family, and indeed the whole community, wrapped their arms around her. This love combined with counseling sessions enabled Gee to begin dealing with the whole situation in a healthy manner. But soon afterward, she was dealt another blow.

A few months after the legal separation, a neighbor who was interested in helping them work things out, visited her husband. While they were talking, her husband mentioned the name of another lady that he had been previously involved with. Gee could hardly believe it when the neighbor called her. "It was like opening a can of worms. I found out that in 1985 while on a truck route through Texas, my husband had entered into a common law marriage with a lady who presently lives in Oklahoma—a relationship he was still involved in. I also found out that in 1995, there was another lady that he began seeing and had been involved with for the past eleven years. By the time I found out about the third lady, I was ready to close the can. I did not want to know about any others."

The disconcerting thing for Gee was that these other ladies knew all about her and her children, but she had no knowledge of them. After the shock wore off, she confronted her husband and he admitted being involved in those relationships while still pledging his love for her. Gee was convinced that he needed psychological help but he maintained that there was nothing wrong with him and that he was fine, psychologically and emotionally.

Desiring to know the whole truth of the situation, Gee contacted the women that her husband had been involved with all those years, and they confirmed her suspicions, sending her pictures and talking openly about situations and events that involved her and her children. There was no doubt in Gee's mind that she had been living a lie. "I had been in a farce of a marriage for twenty-five of the forty-six years that I had been married and that was hard to handle.

I had trusted my husband implicitly, not only was he a Christian, he had been a church leader and an elder for fifteen years."

Gee went through a long period of questioning everything she had ever done in her marriage. Even though her husband kept telling her that it was not her fault, claiming that she had been a perfect wife, she had a hard time not blaming herself.

"I kept spending time in the Word, looking to God to show me the answers to why things had gone so wrong. I finally realized that the guilt was from the devil. I had not done anything to warrant my husband's unfaithfulness all those years. It was he who had done wrong, not me."

Gee had many hours of introspection, looking for clues that she might have missed, clues that could have alerted her to her husband's double life, but came to the conclusion that her only "mistake" was that of being a trusting loving wife.

"God expects a wife to trust her husband and that is all I did. I did not read meanings into the things he said or did and I accepted all his explanations. After all, he was a Christian, a preacher, and an elder."

In 2007 Gee filed for divorce. She had given her husband many opportunities to turn from his infidelity and was willing to forgive him, but he made the choice to live with his mistress and continue in his extra-marital affairs with all those other women.

"I was no longer going to live a lie. Starting life over on my own after 46 years of marriage was the hardest thing I had ever done, but I kept holding onto the fact that God has good thoughts of me and not thoughts of evil. He gave me the strength to cut loose and start again, and today I am making it, stronger than I have ever been before."

Strengthened by the decision she made, Gee moved to another city, closer to her children and grandchildren and made a new life for herself. Today, she is a happy lady, more in love with the Lord than ever before. She has learned much from the many things she went through, but above all, she is even more convinced of the faithfulness of God and has the following advice:

a. As wives, we should be trusting of our husbands, but not naïve. Any suspicions raised in our hearts (by our spirit) should be dealt with lovingly, and in a straightforward manner, bearing in mind that the Spirit will only speak in quietness. "Women today are too busy being moms, wives, workers. We must make time to be quiet in God's presence, for only then will His Spirit speak to us." This discipline goes beyond praying or reading God's Word daily. It involves being quiet long enough to hear Him speak. (Resources that will help in developing a daily quiet time with the Lord are given in the appendix.)

b. We need to trust God's timing for our lives. "I often wonder why I did not learn about my husband's common law marriage earlier until it dawned on me that I could not have found out at a better time. If the divorce had happened earlier, it would have been hard to raise the children on my own without the support of their father." God knows the details of our lives and if we trust His timing, everything will work out to His glory.

c. Some hurts are harder to forgive than others and infidelity is one of the hardest things for the wronged spouse to forgive. The hurt goes to the deepest part of your soul. Gee says, "I prayed over and over that God would help me forgive. I did not want to keep holding this over his head as that gave him too much power over me. I prayed that God would help me let go. I had to realize that forgiveness and reconciliation were two different things. Forgiving did not mean forgetting, it simply meant that remembering was no longer accompanied by the intense hurtful feelings associated with the act. It was important for me to forgive, for how can the Holy Spirit live within our hearts when we harbor bitterness, resentment, and anger?

By forgiving I made an intentional decision no longer to blame, judge or condemn, but to turn his actions and his soul over to God and let Him be the judge." Gee says that remembering kept her faithful as she could see God working in the middle of the whole situation. She admitted that it was a daily battle, but whenever the thought of how badly she had been betrayed would cross her mind, she would hand those thoughts over to God and pray that He would help her forgive. There were days that she would have to do this over and over, sometimes amidst bitter tears.

d. When we go through hurtful situations and loss, it is easy to blame God, especially when we are hurt unfairly. Gee felt such gratitude to God for bringing her husband's unfaithfulness to light that thoughts of blaming Him never crossed her mind. "I had walked with God for so long and because I had a deep relationship with Him, I knew that He is a faithful God and as such, it never crossed my mind to blame Him."

As Christian ladies, we should strive to walk with Him and to deepen our relationship with Him so that when the storms of life blow, our roots will be deep; so deep that though the stem may twist and bend with the fierce winds, we can stand firm and immoveable.

e. God does not promise Christians a life without pain and sorrow but He does promise to walk with us through the hottest fires. We can choose to let life's hurts and disappointments drive us away from Him, or we can choose to use them to deepen our relationship with Him. Gee's pain strengthened her relationship with God. "It made me more dependent on Him. I realized that He was the only one who could give me peace in this situation, so I prayed constantly that He would give me peace and that He would help me forgive. God has answered my prayers as I now have a peaceful and most blessed life in the Lord."

f. We need each other on this journey of life. Gee admits that in addition to her faith in God and prayer, the things that helped her pull through such devastation were the support of her immediate family and the support of her Christian family. There were many days that I could not lift my head off the pillow, but because the saints were praying for me, the strength of their prayers, and their emotional support and love would pick me up and carry me. God in His wisdom gave us the Church as family so that we would have each other to depend on. It is important to be connected to a local congregation that we can call upon at any time, especially when we need others to lean on. Gee prays that her story will help others rely on God and on the support of family and friends when they go through devastating times in life.

Section Review

11. Gee cautions wives to trust their husbands without being naïve. Critically assess your marriage. In what specific ways do you need to draw the line between naivety and trust?

_____

_____

_____

12. Read Matthew 6:14-15 and Mark 11:25-26 in light of Gee's statement, "How can the Holy Spirit live within our hearts when we harbor bitterness, resentment, and anger. The bigger the hurt, the harder it is to forgive, but God requires forgiveness of His children." Who do you need to forgive today?

_____

_____

_____

Write a letter to the Lord about the hurt, handing it over to Him, and asking Him to help you to forgive.

_____

_____

_____

13. Busy lives often make us seem disconnected from members of our Church family. Make a list of three or four women whom you would like to build a relationship with in your congregation. Schedule a time to call them or visit them in the next seven days. Resolve to call or visit at least one of these women weekly for the next month realizing that relationships require an investment of time.

_____

_____

_____

CHAPTER 6

Trusting God Through the Storms of Life (In Light of Eternity)

> The question remains, when life tumbles in, what then? Through our tears, we rest our confidence in one great truth, He who brought us this far will take us safely home.
>
> —Dr. Ray Pritchard

FOR MOST CHILDREN, memories of growing up in a Christian home include laughter, good family times, and a strong feeling of being loved. For Wanda, life as a child was the opposite. She remembers fear and excessive control by her parents, especially by her father. Her most vivid memory of childhood is driving to church as a family, arguing the whole way there and thinking, *Why do we even bother to go to church?* Things at home got worse as she grew older and Wanda could not wait to finish high school and leave home. Many years later, her father was diagnosed with bipolar disease and although this explained his erratic behavior during their childhood, Wanda and her siblings never felt love and affection from him.

After high school, Wanda started college at Troy State and the demands of college were a welcome respite from life at home in Marietta, Georgia. She quickly settled into the routines of college life and was hopeful that four years away from home would heal the scars of growing up in the harsh environment of her childhood. This respite was short-lived as a few months into her sophomore year, Wanda recalls getting a phone call informing her that her brother had been in an automobile accident resulting in severe brain damage and was not expected to live. Her college education came to an unexpected end. Wanda had to move back home.

Those were difficult days, and Wanda remembers that her mother would pray over and over, "Lord, if my son is not in a saved state, please spare his life." She believes strongly that the reason her brother has lived for so many years since the accident, despite the seriousness of his injuries, has been to restore him to a close relationship with God. They have seen God use this situation for His glory.

The brain surgery which her brother had and all the medical expenses involved in his treatment made it financially impossible for Wanda to continue college. And so with a disillusioned heart, she left Troy, went back home, and started working so as to assist her family financially. Although home was the last place Wanda wanted to be, she was grateful that her brother's life had been spared. She faced those days with faith that God would make everything turn out alright. This confidence in God was rewarded just a few months after moving back home when Wanda met the man who would become her husband.

Although only 19 years old, Wanda's life had been so tainted with caution that up to this point she had been unable to commit to any relationship. She says, "It didn't help that growing up, I was not allowed to date. As strict as my father was, he expected us to go to school, come straight home, and stay there till the next morning."

While at Troy, she met a young man and liked him enough to go on dates, but when it appeared the relationship was getting serious, Wanda backed off. "I just could not commit to him. I had an idealistic view of what I wanted in a future husband and nobody I met could fit that ideal." That was until she met her knight in shining armor. She knew from her first few dates that he met all the qualifications she had for a future husband. He was everything that her father had never been—kind, gentle, and affectionate—but her fear of committing to a relationship almost robbed her of this chance at happiness. She recalls letting her fear dominate her. "I had made a list of what I was looking for in a mate and I prayed over this list daily. I could see that this guy met all the qualifications on my list and I knew in my heart that he was chosen by God for me, but I was so afraid."

Her fear resulted in their breaking up and Wanda used the time apart to pray as she had never prayed before. She dreaded being in a marriage like her parents' and thought it better to remain single. It took the guy's patience and his deep relationship with God for Wanda to finally trust God enough to allow herself agree to a commitment. She said, "I came to the realization that I needed to trust God and not allow my fears to ruin my life." This realization made a difference in Wanda's life and less than a year later, she was married.

Barely in her 20's when she got married, Wanda and her husband agreed that they needed to achieve some level of stability before becoming parents, so they decided to wait for at least five years before having children. At the end of those five years, Wanda's fear of not being a good parent re-surfaced and so she asked that they wait five more years. "I was afraid that I would be just like my father. My whole idea of parenting revolved around the dysfunctional family that I had grown up in and I had read just enough books to convince me that awful patterns of child-rearing are easily repeated. I knew for sure that no child should ever go through what my siblings and I went through and I had a fear that I could not break that cycle. My father had since been diagnosed with bipolar disorder and had a serious nervous breakdown. I was afraid this condition was genetic and I could not see myself being a good mother." After fifteen years of marriage, Wanda was so gripped by that fear that she could not envision ever having children.

SECTION REVIEW

1. Often times the things we fear the most keep us from enjoying God's blessings. Wanda almost missed out on being married to a wonderful man because of her fears. In what ways are your fears crippling you and making you miss out on what God has kept for those who love Him? (see 1 Corinthians 2:9)

_____

_____

_____

2. God often works in ways that we do not understand. Having to leave college without completing her education was hard for Wanda, but God had other plans for her. By trusting Him, she allowed Him to fulfill His plans and His will for her life. Read Isaiah 55:8 and write down ways in which God's ways have been very different from what you had planned for your life.

_____

_____

_____

3. It is a known fact that we often repeat the parenting mistakes of our parents with our own kids. One of Wanda's fears was that she would not be a good parent because she had grown up in a dysfunctional family. What are some parenting mistakes that your parents made and what steps are you taking to ensure that you do not repeat the same mistakes with your own children?

_____

_____

_____

4. Often, in spite of our best efforts, we find ourselves repeating the mistakes that our parents make. How does God's grace cover us when we make such mistakes? What makes it easy for us to forgive ourselves and trust that God who sees our hearts and knows our best intentions will ensure that our children thrive regardless of our human frailties?

_____

_____

_____

In her mid-thirties Wanda was forced to make a definite decision about having children. She was diagnosed with fibroid tumors that had to be surgically removed. After the surgery her doctor suggested that if they ever wanted to have children, this was a good time as the fibroids could easily grow back. Wanda wrestled with this decision for a long time. "There were areas of my life in which I had strong faith, but this was one of those areas in which I was so gripped by fear that I could not see straight." At this point, God reached down and met Wanda in her moment of confusion through her sister-in-law who called her one evening and said, "Wanda, you are such a strong person of faith that it is hard for me to believe you are allowing fear to rob you of one of God's richest blessings. The Bible says that children are a blessing from the Lord, why would you let fear keep you from such a blessing?"

Wanda admits that this marked a turning point in her life. She hung up the phone, went immediately to her husband and said, "I have been so wrong because I have not trusted God. I think it is time to stop being afraid and trust God. I want children, you want children, and we have been married fifteen years. I am ready to have children." This conversation brought much needed peace to their hearts and nine months later, Wanda was pregnant. Their faith in God was being rewarded and their joy knew no bounds.

Wanda and her husband excitedly prepared for the birth of their baby. They had waited so long to become parents and resolved that they would be the very best parents that they could be. They began making all the necessary plans that expectant parents make and were overjoyed when five months into the pregnancy, they found out Wanda was pregnant with twins.

Their joy was tinged with anxiety just a month later, when they were informed that there was a problem with one of the baby's brains. They were referred to the Kirkland clinic at University of Alabama at Birmingham (UAB) where the diagnosis was confirmed. Hearing that one of their unborn babies would never have full functionality in her brain was a tremendous blow to them, but their faith was unshaken. Although they had no idea how to care for a baby with such severe disabilities, they both knew that this was their baby and they would love her unconditionally.

The twins were born a few months later, and just as the doctors predicted, one of the newborn baby's conditions was very serious. The first few months were fraught with concerns and anxieties. "During the first month of our baby's life, she stopped breathing many times in a 24-hour period. After six weeks, the doctors asked us to sign a DNR (Do Not Resuscitate) form basically saying that if our baby lost consciousness again, she should not be resuscitated. We were furious, this was our baby and we were not going to allow her to just die."

This refusal to comply with the doctor's instructions was evidence of strong maternal instincts in Wanda. She believed strongly that God had given them this baby for a reason, and they were ready to put up a fight to ensure her survival. At one point, Wanda felt as if the doctors were keeping something from them, so she began pushing for answers. Eventually, an MRI was done and a more serious prognosis was given—their baby had a healthy brain stem but no brain. Since the brain controls all functions, including breathing, they realized that continuously resuscitating their baby was actually torturing her. "It was a very hard decision for us, but my husband and I reached the painful conclusion that maybe her loss of consciousness might be God calling her home and by continuing to resuscitate her, we could have been preventing His will. We decided to sign the DNR and allow God's will to be done."

According to hospital regulations, the baby could only be kept in the hospital for six weeks and the doctors expected her to die before the six weeks were up. To everyone's surprise, she made it through the six weeks and it was time to bring her home. The hospital sent them home with a hospice nurse expecting their baby to die at any minute, but God had other plans for their baby girl. "We got home that first night and were surprised when the hospice nurse refused to leave. We later found out the doctors had told her that our baby would not make it through the night, and she did not want to leave us alone in our moment of loss."

Wanda's baby surprised everybody and it was soon obvious that this baby was a fighter. She not only lived through the night, but was steadily clinging on to life. Wanda and her husband soon settled into a routine of caring for the baby, an exhausting task that drained them emotionally, spiritually, and physically. Wanda remembers waking up many mornings that first year and saying through her tears, "God, I can't do this again today."

The only thing that kept Wanda going was the firm belief that God would see them through this. "I spent many hours reading through the book of Job. I found comfort in the fact that the God who saw Job through his adverse circumstances was our God and that He would see us through. Many times when we were overwhelmed with caring for our baby on our own, God placed some awesome people in our lives. I don't know how we could have made it without some special members of our Church family and my husband's family."

In spite of the physical exhaustion of caring for a severely disabled child while trying to maintain normalcy with the other twin, Wanda admits that the hardest part of the first three years of their daughters' births was trying to make sense of it all. "We had trusted God by finally deciding to have children, and I often felt that He had betrayed that trust. We felt a deep sense of disappointment, especially since we knew He could heal our baby and we did not understand why He didn't."

One of the things that made it easier for Wanda and her husband to deal with the new reality in their family was the open communication that they maintained in their marriage. "Many times I had feelings that nobody else could understand and the only person I could openly share with was my husband. If I had bottled up those feelings, they would have destroyed me and my relationship with God. There was a certain freedom in being able to openly express them to my husband, knowing he could empathize with me without condemning me and this helped us find strength in each other."

Sometimes people who are dealing with stressful situations feel they have to be strong all the time, Wanda and her husband learned the secret of being vulnerable and would often withdraw from others, pour out their grief to the Lord, knowing He was big enough to handle it.

SECTION REVIEW

5. Wanda's faith had earlier led to her laying aside her fears and it now manifested itself when she refused to believe the doctors pronouncement about her baby. She held on to her faith and trust even against obvious circumstances, keeping her eyes fixed on Him. What are some promises of God that keep you going when life does not make sense?

_____

_____

_____

6. In the middle of great trial, Wanda found comfort in reading the book of Job. If you are going through life's troublesome times right now, maybe it is time to visit and spend time with that great man of God, by reading the book of Job. And while there, take a look at this website http://www.keepbelieving.com/sermon/2012-05-05-When-Life-Tumbles-In-What-Then/

List some constructive things that we can do as children of God when He does not do what we know He can do?

_____

_____

_____

7. It is common for hurtful family situations to place an undue burden on the relationship between a husband and wife, leading to strained relationships or even divorce. Wanda's relationship with her husband became stronger through their struggles because they kept communication lines open and took time out to be together. What practical steps can you take to ensure that the problems you are currently facing will draw you and your husband closer instead of apart?

_____

_____

_____

After three years of taking care of their baby at home, John and Wanda made the painful decision to place her in a health care facility. This was another hard decision for them to make, but they realized that as their daughter grew older, she needed more intensive care than they could provide at home. They also realized that they needed to devote time to caring for their other daughter, so they prayed and waited for the Lord to direct them. A few months after asking God to show them what to do, they were led to a health care facility that met their needs. "We have enjoyed and embraced our daughter's second home, visiting her constantly, making her an integral part of our lives and watching her and her sister develop a special closeness."

Wanda has seen God lead and direct every aspect of her life, from choosing the right job for her, one that allowed her to spend as much time caring for her babies as she needed, to making health decisions about where to place her daughter. "It is easy to spend our time on this earth questioning God and why He allows certain things to happen in our lives. I have realized that when things do not make sense, it is because we are looking at life based on our earthly expectations. Things look quite different when viewed in light of eternity. God has a definite purpose for our being here, and if everything we go through is to bring Him glory, then it is all worth it."

Just when Wanda had settled into a routine that allowed her to balance caring for her daughters, her job, and her role as a wife and a daughter to aging parents, she was diagnosed with Parkinson's disease. She recalls the day the prognosis was made, noting that instead of falling apart in tears, it was easy for her to accept it because, "In light of eternity, this diagnosis was nothing." Wanda knows that her illness is a degenerative one, but her face still sparkles with joy and peace. "God brought me to this earth and nothing that happens to me takes Him by surprise. I will continue to love Him, praise Him, and glorify Him as long as He gives me breath."

In the past few years, Wanda has gone through surgery and various tests; she has seen her disease take a turn for the worse and is currently considering brain surgery to reverse some of the effects of the disease. Her faith is as strong now as ever. "I know He is the great physician and until He decides to heal this body, I will keep on trusting Him; for when I am weak, then I am strong"

Some of the things that stand out in Wanda's life as she has gone through all the situations she has faced are:

a. The strong conviction that we are here to glorify God, not to have a perfect life. Wanda says, "God expects us to see all things in light of eternity, and if we do, then everything we are going through on life's journey eventually makes sense." When things do not turn out the way we would want them to, all we have to do is trust God and believe that everything will be alright.

b. Wanda admits unashamedly the belief that God directly intervenes in the lives of His children as much today as He did in Bible days. Her life has been filled with examples of such interventions, with God sometimes revealing things to her in dreams and sometimes giving her a strong sense of intuition. One example she readily gives is the dream she had before she was pregnant. She recalls having a dream in which she was fighting for the lives of her unborn children, and in that dream she was told that everything was going to be okay. She also recalls having a strong feeling about moving their daughter from one health care center to another and asking God for signs of confirmation. The signs were sent to her in undeniable ways, so she went ahead and removed their daughter. It was only after removing her that they found out all the underlying problems that the previous facility had, and Wanda was grateful that she had listened to the nudging in her spirit.

c. Wanda has great admiration and love for her mother-in-law. She admits that she has learned about sacrificial love and selfless living from her husband's mother and recalls the day she met the lady that would become her mother-in-law. It was on a Sunday morning and Wanda went to Church like she always did. She noticed that there was a visitor sitting in one of the back pews by herself, so she introduced herself and asked permission to sit with her during the worship service. During the announcements, prayer requests were made for Jay Holland who was still in critical condition and not expected to live. The lady noticed that the last name was the same as Wanda's and asked if they were related. "With tears in my eyes, I told her he was my brother, and I will never forget how she put her arms around my shoulders, spoke peace to my heart, and told me that everything would be alright, if I only believed. She did not know how much turmoil I had been under, but her touch and her calm demeanor made a tremendous difference in my perspective and I felt like a heavy weight was lifted from me."

After church, Wanda went home relieved in her Spirit and with a deep conviction that she had met an angel and that her brother would be okay. After dating her husband for months, he arranged for her to meet his mom, and her first reaction when she recognized her as the lady who had spoken peace to her heart that day in church was, "She can't be your mom, she is an angel!" After more than twenty-three years of marriage, Wanda still calls her mother-in-law an angel.

d. Life does not always make sense but it doesn't have to. Our Father rules from above and He has a good and perfect will for us. It does not make sense to dwell on the unfairness that we perceive, but rather, may our eyes be opened to realize that every good and perfect gift comes from above (James 1:17). In spite of how difficult things may be, we can praise Him for the good days, the good friends, the supportive spouse, the loving church family, and so on. We must make a choice to lift our eyes beyond this life and know that in eternity, it will all make sense.

e. Our reactions to the things we go through is largely a result of what we consciously decide to focus on. It is easy to focus on the hardships of life, but Wanda chooses to focus on the positive. She says, "I know we have gone through a lot, but it could have been worse. I choose to focus on how God has blessed us through our trials, knowing that everybody has their own trials and my current reality is mine. I choose to deal with that reality in a way that will glorify God."

f. Wanda derives her strength from the Word of God. In the midst of her greatest struggles, she would sit for hours reading the book of Job and would draw comfort from the struggles he went through. "I realize that life does not always have a happy ending. John the Baptist was beheaded and Uriah the Hittite was murdered, but God is always in control. Reading about the emotions that others in the scriptures went through always gives me comfort and hope." There is no greater discipline in the life of a Christian than the discipline of daily Bible reading/study. We do not have to wait until life throws us a curve before we dig into the Word, for rainy days are sure to come. The difference between one who sings in the rain and one who sees only the bleak, heavy clouds, lies in a lifetime spent reading the Word daily.

SECTION REVIEW

8. The Bible tells us in Hebrews 13:2 that it is possible for humans to meet angels and not be aware of who these celestial beings are. Describe an incident in your life in which you were convinced you had met an angel and how that incident affected you.

_____

_____

_____

9. We often carry our past into our present and allow it to negatively affect our decisions. Paul claims that he always tried to forget "those things which are behind and reach forward to those things that are ahead" (Philippians 3:13). What hurts of the past are you still holding onto and how is this affecting your present and possibly your future?

_____

_____

_____

10. What practical steps can be taken to let go of the past and embrace the blessings that we have in Christ Jesus.

_____

_____

_____

11. A Christian perspective requires that every situation we face be considered "in light of eternity." What are the situations in your life that you need to apply this perspective to?

_____

_____

_____

CHAPTER 7

Lessons From the Depression Era That Transcend Generation and Culture Part 1
(Keep Your Feet Moving Until He Tells You to Stop)

I have learned throughout my life that complete dependence upon God always pays; I have seen Him providing every need, whether here in America, in Asia, or faraway in Africa.
—Grace Farrar

THE DEPRESSION WAS a difficult period in the history of the United States and growing up then was very hard. For Grace, the third child in a family of four, born on a farm in southern Indiana in the 1930's, life was hard, but fun. She recalls endless days of churning milk into butter, growing everything they ate, and going to school in a one-room school house. The lessons she learned during those days have stayed with her all her life. "I have always thanked God for growing up during the depression as it taught us to appreciate everything we had and we learned how to 'make do.'"

Grace admits that many of the things she had to do (much later in her life), as a pioneer missionary's wife in Tanzania and Nigeria, were things she had learned to do in those early years during the depression. She recalls washing and grinding wheat in Tanzania, using the chaff to make breakfast cereal and the fine parts for flour. Chores that made life on the mission field almost unbearable for other ladies were a delight for her, as the foundation for coping had been laid early in her life.

At age five, Grace had a strong desire for learning and was allowed to go to school with her older siblings. Although the plan was for her to sit in on the classes until she turned six, Grace's academic ability was noticed by the visiting superintendent who directed that she should be formally enrolled in the school, despite her age. Grace officially became a student at five years of age, loved learning, and later became the valedictorian of her class, following in the footsteps of her older siblings who had also been valedictorians of their classes. "My mother made learning fun. Since we did not have a television set, every evening was spent with mother (who had a ninth-grade education) reading aloud to us. She alternated between reading the classics and reading Bible stories. These stories enriched us, expanded our minds, and created in us an eagerness to learn."

SECTION REVIEW

1. As parents, our desire is to make life easy for our children. Sometimes we do this by doing everything for them and taking away all responsibilities from them. What are some age appropriate household responsibilities/chores that need to be taught to our children so as to lay a proper foundation of hard work and responsibility?

_____

_____

_____

2. Our generation relies heavily on the television, computers, and video games for entertainment and education of our children, often with disastrous results. What family traditions can we initiate that would enrich our children, expand their minds, and create in them an eagerness to learn?

_____

_____

_____

Grace finished high school in 1942 and was ready to pursue her dream of being a nurse. Although no one in her family had ever gone to college, and even though at the time the country was at the tail end of the depression, Grace was not deterred from following her dream. She knew that her parents would not be able to afford the cost of higher education for her, so she made plans to get a job. Her goal was to save enough money to pay her way through nursing school.

The day after high school graduation, Grace left home and moved in with her sister, who had earlier gotten married and was expecting her second child. She got her first job in an ice-cream shop, making $10.00 a week. Mindful of her goal, she spent her tips and saved all of her paycheck. In ten weeks she was able to pay $50.00 tuition fee (for the three years of training in a nursing program), $20.00 for uniforms, $25.00 for books, and $5.00 for a watch with which to check the pulse and heart rate of her patients! That left her without any spending money, but Grace was where she wanted to be and she depended on God to provide for her needs.

The first year of nursing school was demanding but fun and Grace loved every minute of it. At the end of her second year, the government began a cadet nursing program—a program which trained nurses for World War II, paid all their school expenses, and gave them an allowance of $20.00 a week. Joining the cadets would mean moving from Indiana to Cincinnati, a big move for Grace, but she knew that it would give her relief from the financial burden of nursing school, so she applied to the program, was accepted, and began her training as a military nurse in 1944. Although she was in the program for only a year, the training Grace received in the cadet nursing program taught her a principle for living—a principle which became a philosophy of life for her.

"We had this old Sergeant who would take us through all kinds of drills. Once during a drill, we marched and marched until we reached a wall and then we stopped. I remember him barking at us 'Why did you stop?' At the time, I wondered if he expected us to go through the wall, and then he barked, 'You are supposed to keep your feet moving until I say halt.'"

"I later realized how good a motto that was and decided that I would always keep my feet moving, even when I reached a dead end, until the Lord told me to halt." This philosophy of life laid a foundation that Grace built on for the rest of her life.

Grace finished the nursing program a year later and received her diploma. The war ended soon after, releasing the cadet nurses from their obligation to the government. Grace was free to practice her nursing skills wherever she wanted. She chose to work in a hospital in Cincinnati.

While in her senior year of nursing school, Grace visited her roommate's church, a small congregation of the Church of Christ in Cincinnati. Her family had devoutly attended a community church, but by the time she moved to the city and began nursing school, she found out that "a country church was very different from city church" and became very uncomfortable with the ritualistic nature of the community church in the city. By the time she was a senior in nursing school, she had stopped going to church altogether. One day, on her roommate's invitation, Grace visited a nearby Church of Christ, and it was readily apparent that this church was different from any other church she had been to before. "The first time I went with my roommate, I realized that this church was focused on following the Bible. I felt God's Word tugging at my heart and I began to study the Bible like never before. I was so convicted by the things I read that a week after my first visit, I was baptized and became a Christian at the age of twenty."

The summer after Grace's baptism, a group of students from Harding University came to work with the congregation, and meeting them rekindled the desire for a college education in Grace's heart. She knew she could not afford to pay for college, but her new philosophy of "keeping your feet moving'" propelled her and so she sent letters to about five Christian colleges, stating her desire to go to college and her lack of resources to finance that desire. She was discouraged by the responses of all the colleges with the exception of Harding University. Dean Sears of Harding took time to reply to Grace's letter, not just applauding her desire for further education, but stating the possibility of her being employed as a nurse at a local hospital while going to Harding. He promised to assist in arranging her class schedule to favor such employment. And so it was that Grace saved $60.00 during that summer and by the fall of 1946 she boarded a train, "The Missouri Pacific," on her way to college, the first person in her family to get a college education.

SECTION REVIEW

3. Grace was driven by a dream that was larger than her and she took definitive steps to fulfill that dream. What dreams do you have for this season of your life and what can you do intentionally to get on the path towards fulfilling that dream?

_____

_____

_____

4. Grace's philosophy of life was formed from her encounter with a drill Sergeant during her training as a cadet nurse. Take time to think of one or two people who have crossed your path and who have positively impacted you and write their names below. Write a note to each of them this week (or make a quick phone call), expressing appreciation for their influence on your life.

_____

_____

_____

5. Grace was not deterred by the obstacles on her path toward a college education, but kept her feet moving. What obstacles are currently blocking your view and how can you decisively work towards removing those obstacles?

_____

_____

_____

Because of the credits earned in nursing school, Grace entered college as a junior. College was everything she had thought it would be—demanding and exhausting—but Grace loved every part of it. By the time she had taken a few classes, Grace decided to use her background in nursing for a medical career and declared a pre-med major. Working 7 P.M. to 7 A.M. in the nearby hospital as a night supervisor allowed her to be on campus for her 8 A.M. class, but it was a rigorous schedule. Grace kept her focus on achieving her desire of a college education, and that first semester she had a 4.0 GPA.

By the beginning of the second semester, the college nurse resigned and the university president offered Grace the position of college nurse. This was a prayer answered and resulted in a less rigorous schedule. During her second year as a pre-med student, Grace started to rethink her choice of medicine as a career. "At that time, all the female medical doctors I knew seemed to devote their whole time to the medical profession, and that was not what I wanted. I wanted to have a family. I wanted to be a wife and a mother. Having enough time to raise my children was important to me, so I changed my major to home economics." With her diploma in nursing, Grace continued working as the college nurse and the change in major gave her more time to actually enjoy being a college student.

While in a chemistry class in her junior year, Grace sat next to a student named Henry, and before long they realized that they had similar backgrounds. Just like Grace, he was the first one in his family to go to college and he was also working to pay his way through school. Henry was the student instructor assigned to assist students in biology laboratories, and Grace and he quickly became good friends. He had dreams of being a medical missionary and was determined to make that dream come true.

A year after they became friends, Henry left Harding University to finish his last year of pre-medical education at UT Knoxville as a pre-requisite for admission to medical school. Grace knew she was losing a good friend, but was thankful that their paths had crossed. She had no way of knowing that God had other plans for the two of them.

As the college nurse, Grace was often assisted by student workers who did most of the clean-up jobs and she remembers the day that one of her student workers told her how much she admired a guy named Henry. "When she told me how she had always wanted to date him, upset that he had left Harding, I quickly replied that I knew him and would write to him about her. I found Henry's address, wrote to him, and told him what a nice person this girl was, encouraging him to correspond with her."

"Henry replied almost immediately. But to my great shock, his reply was not about the girl, but rather about his feelings for me! After I got over the shock, I wrote him back, and we started regular communications." These communications led to their falling in love and a marriage proposal and in December of 1950, Grace and Henry were married. They happily settled into married life, excited about their future as a medical missionary and a medical missionary's wife.

Before they were married, Henry had been told by the congregation that had promised to support his medical school education that they could no longer sponsor him. The congregation needed a bigger church building and this appeared to be a higher priority than training a future medical missionary. In desperation, Henry went to graduate school and obtained a master's degree in parasitology, but that only fueled his desire for medical school, so he applied again to UT Knoxville Medical School.

Grace remembers that they had no means of paying for her husband's medical school education. "When Henry was admitted again to UT Knoxville and realized that we could not afford it, he considered seeking employment as a teacher instead. I knew this would mean giving up a long-sought after dream and I refused to let him do it. I told him that his desire to be a medical missionary would glorify God and bring relief to many people. I encouraged him not to give up, but to trust that God would make a way. Based on my philosophy of keeping one's feet moving, I urged him to begin medical school and let God worry about his fees."

"By the time we got married in December 1950, Henry was set to start medical school in January 1951. We had no idea where the money would come from for him to start school, but we were moving by faith." Henry began medical school, and Grace started working as a private nurse. The couple did not know how they would be able to afford the quarterly tuition fee of $125.00 for medical school, but God was faithful. Every time tuition was due, they were able to pay, many times at the last minute and often through the generosity of friends and family members. Henry also worked in a hospital laboratory and they saved as much money as they could.

Grace recalls the last year of Henry's medical education when they needed more money than usual for medical supplies and examination fees and they just could not save enough money. They were set against borrowing, but it appeared as if that was their last resort. Henry told Grace that their only option was to take out a student loan and that being his last semester, he would get a job after graduation and easily pay back the $300.00 loan that they needed.

This was the last thing Grace wanted them to do, but she reluctantly agreed. With a despondent heart and shuffling steps, Henry walked into the office the next day to ask for a loan application form. He was told that the Pfizer Company had just given $1,000 as a grant to be divided among three senior medical students, and that since he qualified for the grant, it would provide the $300.00 he needed and they would not need to borrow after all! To their surprise and joy, Henry was able to finish medical school without owing anything. It was another great evidence of God's providence.

Grace recounts another situation when she saw God's amazing providence. Her family, now including two children, had just moved to Tampa, Florida, for Henry's internship. Everything they had as a family was loaded into one vehicle. She had a crib for her older child who was eighteen months old but needed another one for the one-month-old baby. She recalls saving as much as she could from the $100.00 that her husband was paid monthly for the crib.

Just as she eventually saved the $20.00 that she needed, Henry was involved in an accident on his way back from church one morning when he went off the road to avoid a collision and hit a telephone pole. Although there were no injuries, the car needed some repairs and the $20.00 went toward making those repairs. Giving up her crib money was easy for Grace because she knew God would provide, although she did not know just how He would do it. A few days after the accident, the story of the poor intern who used his baby's crib money for car repairs spread around the hospital, and a medical doctor invited her husband to his house. He led Henry to his garage where he had stored the baby furniture used for his twins who were now grown up. He offered them any furniture they needed, so instead of just a crib, Henry left that man's house with a crib, a high chair, a play pen, a stroller, and all kinds of baby furniture. God had come through for them again.

The time in Tampa went by fast, and Henry finished his internship. During this time the Korean conflict began and the doctor's draft law required that medical doctors serve for two years. Henry requested that he be allowed to serve in the country so as to take care of his young family and he was assigned to medical centers in Texas and in North Carolina. After his two-year service, he began his surgical residency in Harlan, Kentucky, and completed it in Winston-Salem, North Carolina.

In 1960, Henry's surgical training was completed and it was time to make future plans. The family had grown to include three more children, and everybody was excited about which foreign country God would lead them to. Grace felt as if everything she had gone through her whole life had been to prepare her for this. She could feel doors opening for her and her family. Although she had no idea where those doors would lead, she had learned to trust in Him who knows the end of all things from its very beginning. She had learned lessons that would serve as solid foundations for her and her family and could hardly wait to see how those lessons would serve them in the future that God had for them.

Section Review

6. The faith that Grace had in God's ability to provide led her to encourage her husband to pursue his dream of being a medical doctor, when he would so easily have given up. Often, my role as a wife involves encouraging my husband with a quiet and meek spirit. Read 1 Peter 3:1-4 and write down a few areas that your husband might need some encouragement today. In what practical ways will you provide that encouragement?

_____

_____

_____

7. It was easy for Grace to trust God and give up her baby's crib money because she had seen him provide for them many times before. Sometimes current difficult situations make it easy to forget how God has worked in our lives in the past. Make a list of five ways that God has proved His faithfulness to you and your family in the past few months. Pause and thank Him for those even as you pray for His grace in your current situation.

_____

_____

_____

8. Standing at the brink of new experiences can be both scary and exciting. The exhilaration of being in new situations, meeting new people, and embarking on a new journey can easily be dampened by our love for *status quo*. What new situation are you facing or about to face right now? Write down some of the reasons that this new situation appears so scary.

_____

_____

_____

CHAPTER 8

Lessons From the Depression Era That Transcend Generation and Culture Part 2
(Keep Your Feet Moving Until He Tells You to Stop)

Where can I go from your Spirit? Or where can I flee from your presence? If I ascend into heaven, You are there; ... if I take the wings of the morning ... even there Your hand shall lead me, and Your right hand shall hold me.

—Psalm 139:7-10

AS THEY SOUGHT the Lord's direction for their lives, Grace and Henry considered going to India as medical missionaries, but at that time, India was only open to people from the commonwealth countries. They considered China, but China was controlled by the communists and so entry by Christian missionaries was restricted.

As they continued praying about where God would have them serve, they received a letter from missionaries in Nigeria complaining about their inability to preach the Gospel because of health issues they had to deal with in that country. Patti and Rees Bryant, college friends of Henry and Grace, ended their letter by asking, "Where are our Christian doctors when we need them?" This was just the invitation they needed.

After a series of preparations, Grace, her husband, and their five children, boarded a plane to serve the Lord in Nigeria. Grace allowed her adventurous spirit to take over, grateful that their dream of serving the Lord in a foreign country was finally being fulfilled. She admits to trusting God completely and not harboring any reservations about raising her children in a different culture, far away from family and friends.

"God had proven Himself faithful to us in many ways, and I had no doubt that He would take control of whatever situations we would face in Africa. The children had always known what our family's mission was, so there was an air of excitement among all of us as we began the journey that would change our lives forever."

Henry had barely settled in when he saw the need for a medical clinic that would serve the people of southeastern Nigeria. Working with other doctors in the government hospitals in the area only served to show him how poorly medicine was practiced, and he began to nurse the desire of establishing a clinic that would be operated on Christian principles. The first challenge was that of finding a suitable building. Although Henry was interested in converting an old building that had once served as a guest house for British officers during the colonial days, the task of obtaining government permission for the use of the building was a long and difficult one.

Once approval was given to use the building, the protocol for establishing a clinic was arduous, especially when initiated by a foreigner. Grace fought these battles on her knees as she had fought all her previous battles and after a year of filing papers and attending interviews, approval was given for establishing the clinic. The initial hurdles were over, but greater obstacles arose, including the need for qualified personnel and the financial demands involved in putting up buildings and buying equipment.

Two nurses from the United States came to Nigeria and began recruiting girls from nearby villages to train as nurse's aides. Grace recalls the difficult task of training student nurses who had grown up on dirt floors. Although these girls knew nothing about aseptic techniques and the dangers associated with bacteria and contamination of surfaces and wounds, she was astonished at their willingness to learn. Their desire to improve the living conditions of their people made them the best nurse's aides she had ever worked with.

After being there for two years, approval was given for a full-fledged hospital and construction work began on buildings which would serve as the wards. Another test of faith came when it was time to equip the wards. There were some in Henry's supporting congregation who believed strongly that a church could not scripturally support a medical doctor or give contributions to any type of medical work. In their minds, the mission work of the church was restricted to evangelism and soul winning. This resulted in the congregation agreeing to support Him as a "preaching physician" and required that Henry would have to balance his duties as preacher and physician. This meant preaching in the market squares and establishing local congregations while serving as the chief surgeon for the newly-established hospital. It also meant that Grace and her husband had to look to other sources for financial assistance in equipping the wards.

She admits seeing God work through many brethren all over the United States who sent in money regularly to support the medical work that was done in Nigeria. Worthy of mention were the large donations made by Brother F.F. Carson of Richmond, California, and the outreach initiated by Patti Bryant's mother in Lubbock, Texas. She wrote letters asking people to donate $10.00 per bed for the maternity wards. Enough money was raised from this outreach that it not only provided enough beds, but was enough to provide all the equipment that was needed for the ward.

Grace remembers the day they ran out of money to pay construction workers and they had to suspend work at the construction site. Telling the workers there was no more money to continue the work, she and her husband went home, discouraged. She recalls thinking that if God wanted the building completed, He would make a way, so she refused to give in to hopelessness. As she and Henry sat down that evening to open the day's mail, one of the letters contained a check for a several thousand dollars from Brother Carson. This was another evidence of God's provision when it appeared all hope was lost. They used it as a testimony of God's faithfulness as they called the workers back the very next day. Grace had learned all through her life that a life of dependence upon God always pays and she saw God providing every need, even when she was eight thousand miles away in a foreign continent.

SECTION REVIEW

1. Sometimes we feel that God is too far removed from our current situation to be of help. Grace saw him use different people in different ways to intervene in situations that she faced in Africa. Make a list below of some people that God has caused you to meet in the past few weeks to bless you. Send a thank you letter to one or more of them this week.

_____

_____

_____

2. Grace's faith made it easy for her to leave her country and work among the people of Africa sharing God's love and impacting their faith. We may not be called to go overseas on account of our faith, but we are expected to impact those we meet daily for the Lord. Write down two ways that you will intentionally reach out to a neighbor or an acquaintance this week.

_____

_____

_____

3. Life in Africa required a total dependence on God's ability and willingness to provide for every need. Past experiences had strengthened Grace's faith and dependence. What struggles are you currently facing that require a total dependence on God and how can such dependence be developed?

_____

_____

_____

Grace admits that the women of Nigeria easily captured her heart and were a great source of encouragement to her. She remembers many days when the women, who wanted a hospital so badly, would show up at construction sites, after a full day of working as farmers or traders in the local markets. They would come in large groups with babies strapped to their backs and would clear the land alongside the men, singing the whole time. It was obvious that they were tired of their children dying from diseases that could easily be prevented and were willing to do anything to assist in building the hospital.

Although traditionally, it was the man's duty to clear the land, these women dispensed with tradition, wielding machetes alongside their men, doing all they could to show their appreciation of these "foreigners" who loved them enough to make life easier and better for them and their families.

Three years went by quickly, and the hospital started functioning and catering to the medical needs of the people. Grace and her family were settling down and beginning to feel at home in Nigeria, when the Nigerian civil war of 1967 began. The American Government ordered wives and children out of Nigeria. Grace reluctantly left her husband and went to Lagos, the capital city of Nigeria.

Arriving in Lagos with other Americans, who almost exclusively were employees of oil companies and other huge establishments, Grace watched as each person was picked up by representatives from their companies and taken away to hotels and other arranged accommodations. She was the only missionary family on the plane, and no arrangements had been made for her. She had been given the name and phone number of a company in Lagos, but could not get through to them. They were not expecting her. She recalls being at the airport until it started to get dark. She didn't have enough money for food or for a taxi cab, and even if she could afford a cab, she had nowhere to take her children. The children started asking "What are we going to do, now, Mom?" and the only answer Grace had was one she had given them often, "Let's just wait and see what the Lord has in store for us." Instead of giving in to fear and despair, Grace knew that this would be another opportunity for God to show His awesome presence and power.

Eventually, she and her children were the last people in the terminal, and the airport official approached her asking who she was and where she was going. She gave the number of her contact person to the official, not knowing what would happen if they got through to the person on the other end. Grace recalls hearing the official say, "We have a lady with five children here at the airport," and to her surprise the voice on the other end said, "Tell her we are on our way to pick her up. We have been expecting her."

Grace could hardly believe it, but a few minutes later, a limousine from an oil company pulled up, and they were driven to the home of an oil company executive who was in America at the time, but had made his home available to any missionary family that needed it. She and her children were taken to a beautiful home where they were taken care of until they left Nigeria. Grace's faith in God's provision had paid off again.

The war in Nigeria became more severe, and it was not long before the American Government ordered all Americans out of Nigeria. Grace and the children could no longer stay in Lagos waiting for her husband to join them, so, based on an agreement she had earlier made with her husband, they flew to Rome and stayed in a local hotel arranged for them by missionaries. A few days later, her husband joined them in Rome, and together they went back to the United States.

Feeling that their work in Nigeria had ended prematurely, especially since they left Nigeria barely two years after being given permission to open the Nigerian Christian Hospital, her husband looked for every opportunity to return to Nigeria after the civil war. Such opportunity came when USAID and Kaiser International got a contract to reactivate the General Hospital in Port Harcourt, Nigeria. Because of his previous experience with medical care in Nigeria, Henry became the leader of the medical team and the family moved back to Nigeria for two years. This gave them the chance to oversee surgery and health care in the Nigerian Christian Hospital, Onicha Ngwa, a project they had started before the civil war in 1967.

After two years there, Grace and her husband were ready to return to the United States. Their services as a medical missionary husband-wife team did not end when they returned from Nigeria, but God opened doors for them in countries like Tanzania and China. Grace is quick to say that her greatest challenge in mission work was in China where she and her husband were the first set of Christians to be admitted as teachers of English as a second language.

While it is illegal to proselytize in China, they went as English teachers and could answer any questions that the students asked about Christianity. Many of the students they worked with were medical students who were preparing for graduate work in America, so their job was to familiarize these students with American English instead of the British English to which they had been exposed. Grace went beyond what was expected of her and taught them about American customs, the American banking system, and how to write scientific papers. Ministering to communist China, within the bounds of the law, while portraying Jesus, was an opportunity that still remains memorable in her mind.

Grace has had a tremendous impact on medical missions in Nigeria. In 2009, in her eighties, she made her last trip to Nigeria. She still recalls the warm welcome given to her and her husband by the people of southeast Nigeria. During that last visit, Grace and her husband, mindful of the needs of the Nigerian people initiated a bore-hole project that would give water to the whole village. The project was completed by the end of that year and is a lasting testimony to the love of these pioneer Nigerian missionaries.

Grace believes that raising her children largely in foreign countries contributed immensely to what her children have grown up to be—children with a Christian worldview, who are following in their parent's footsteps. Presently, all six children are married with children of their own, and Grace is a blessed grandmother of six grandchildren. She admits that she took the task of raising her children very seriously because like Hannah, she was aware that the children belonged more to the Lord than to her. Tracing her own faith back to her mother's faith, Grace intentionally nurtured her children in their spiritual walk and is a little concerned that today's mothers do not take this responsibility as seriously as they should. Grace advises mothers to "be intentional about training your children in the way of the Lord. Bring God into every conversation, be quick to thank Him for every blessing, but above all, spend time with your kids, reading Bible stories to them or teaching them from God's Word."

Section Review

4. Proverbs 29:15 says that a child left to himself brings his mother to shame, implying the responsibility of mothers in the upbringing of their children. What changes need to be made so that more time is spent by you on the spiritual nurturing of your children?

_____

_____

_____

5. The following are personal suggestions for increasing spiritual awareness in our children:

   a. Bring God readily into conversations.
   b. Creatively engage children in Bible story times at home.
   c. Have daily family devotionals.
   d. Ensure that each child has a daily private quiet time, sitting quietly in God's presence for a fixed amount of time, depending on the age of the child, or reading and meditating on His Word.
   e. Encourage them to talk to God about everything.
   f. Find creative and fun ways to be accessible to each child.
   g. Ensure that conversations about God focus on His omnipotence, His omnipresence, and His abiding love.

Discuss how you will intentionally incorporate these suggestions into daily routines with your child.

Grace's life has been the epitome of a life lived under God's wonderful canopy of grace and providence. Urged by other missionary wives eager to learn from her experiences, Grace wrote her memoirs down in a book titled, *Stand By and See What the Lord Will Accomplish*, published in 2002. Thereafter, she settled down to enjoy being a full time wife and grandmother. In 2010, life dealt her a cruel blow when her husband of sixty years died unexpectedly. She recalls her husband's last days after the fall that led to paralysis and his eventual death. His last day on earth was on a Sunday, and he was on life support with his family surrounding him. They had made arrangements for him to partake of the Lord's Supper as that was something he had never missed since his baptism at eleven years of age.

The family spent the day singing around his bedside as he quietly slipped out of this earthly plane to his eternal reward. Grace admits that what has kept her going has been a complete reliance on God, a reliance and dependence that she had cultivated over the years. When people ask her what her plans are now that Henry is gone, the answer that comes readily to her lips is, "I am going to take it one day at a time, like I have always done." Her advice to Christian women who find themselves in the same situation is to take the focus off of themselves and their loss. With a twinkle in her eye she says, "My husband has reached the goal he set for himself and has gone home to be with the Lord. I cannot grieve for him. Surely, if I were grieving, I would only grieve for me. The Lord must still have something He wants me to do here or I would have left also. Of course, I miss him daily, but I rely on the Lord, knowing He will re-unite us in His own good time, and I take it one day at a time."

Her love for writing keeps her occupied and she sets aside specific times during the week to write letters to her granddaughters, two of whom are away in college. Friends, women prisoners in Texas, and members of her local congregation are all a part of her mail ministry. She has a joy for living that keeps her focused on reaching out to others as she lives one day at a time until the Lord returns or calls her home. In her late eighties, Grace admits that if she had to live life all over again, she would not change a single thing. "I have done more than I ever dreamed I would do. I give God all the glory for a wonderful life." Like Paul, she has fought the good fight and run the race and is waiting to receive the crown which God has kept for her. Where Grace is, is where we all long to be.

SECTION REVIEW

6. Grace admits that her source of strength has been faith in God and what He is able to do. Take time this week to read about those listed in the "faith hall of fame" in Hebrews chapter 11. Make notes on those characters that inspire your faith walk.

_____

_____

_____

7. One of the secrets of Grace's successful life as a widow has been the fact that she easily sees things that need to be done and gets busy doing them. She says, "There are people to pray for, letters to send, people that I can sit with for a while—always something that needs to be done." Sometimes we focus on our needs and our own problems and this keeps us from reaching out. Look in your neighborhood and among your church family and pray that God will open your eyes to a need that you can

fulfill. Write down below the people and the need He brings to your heart. Resolve today to "be about your Father's business" and let the Lord work on meeting your own needs.

_____

_____

_____

8. Grace admits that life can only be meaningful when one has a close personal relationship with God—a life that meditates on the Word, constantly. Her favorite passage of scripture is Philippians 4:6: "Be careful for nothing; but in everything by prayer and supplication with thanksgiving let your requests be made known unto God" (KJV). It is often easy to focus on our struggles and take our blessings for granted. Make a list of all the things you are thankful for—no matter how small they seem. Lay your hand on this list and thank God for these things daily for the next few days.

_____

_____

_____

CHAPTER 9

Surrendering All to Him Who Knows Best

I believe the key to surrendering all is not to start when times are bad, but to build a continual relationship with God that will support you when times get bad. Learning to surrender in the middle of a great storm is a hard feat, but habit will make you hold on to something that makes you feel secure. Learning to surrender early in your Christian walk makes all the difference.

—Dee

GROWING UP IN a Christian home was everything that it should be for Dee. She grew up as a preacher's kid, with a sister and two brothers, moving from city to city wherever her father had a preaching job. At eighteen years of age, she attended David Lipscomb University where she majored in speech communication and public relations.

Graduating from Lipscomb, Dee was ready to settle into a career in broadcasting or any field relevant to her major, but admits that God obviously had other plans for her. She immediately settled into an alternative career path, but a few years into her career, Dee was ready for marriage.

"I was a good girl, saving myself for the man that God would one day bring my way. I was industrious and fun loving, believing without any doubt that I would be a good wife to some good husband. I was established in my career, had my own apartment, my own car, and was comfortable with my life and myself. I was in a good space where I was ready to spend the rest of my life building a Christian family."

Almost immediately God brought a Christian young man into Dee's life. They easily fell in love and were married within two years of meeting each other. Like her, her husband had grown up in the church, so it was natural for him to become a leader in their local congregation. They became very involved in serving God and their church family, and everyone loved them and saw them as the ideal Christian couple. Dee became pregnant with a baby boy and her life was becoming perfect as she looked forward to being a Christian mother and building an idyllic Christian family.

This state of perfection did not last long, for Dee found out during her pregnancy that her husband had been unfaithful to her. This was very hard for her to handle. She had been a great wife, loving her husband, being there for him in all the ways that mattered. She could not understand what had gone wrong. Being leaders in the church had led to great expectations from both of them, and although neither of them was perfect, infidelity was the last thing Dee would have expected from her husband.

After unsuccessfully trying to find out how things could have gone so wrong, Dee began slowly to deal with the heartache accompanying marital infidelity, hoping that her marriage could be saved.

Within the next three years it became obvious that her husband was no longer interested in the marriage. Dee watched her marriage fall apart as they decided to file for divorce. "I had to learn to surrender. For the first time in my life I felt that I was not completely in control. Life was not turning out the way it was supposed to for a good Christian girl who had served God all her life, maintained her chastity until marriage, and married a Christian." For the longest time, Dee kept asking God why this had happened. "Over and over, I kept asking, what did I miss Lord? He was a Christian man, we both went to church. We both sought to serve you together. What did I miss? Of course to this day, there have been no answers, and I have learned to leave it alone and stop questioning." One way Dee learned to let go of the past was by asking God to help her forget, and she is thankful that in His mercy, He has not only lessened the hurt feelings behind that first failed marriage, but has literally erased it almost completely from her memory.

Dee poured herself into raising her son as a single parent, with the support of her immediate family and her church family. She filled his childhood with wonderful experiences. Her joy came from watching him grow into a well-adjusted little boy with a strong sense of security in who he was and in God's love for him.

It took many more years for Dee to learn to trust again, but eventually, she met and fell in love with a good Christian young man. As would be expected, she entered into this new relationship with tremendous caution, not only guarding her heart, but protecting her son. She spent many hours in prayer, desiring to enter into another relationship ONLY if it was God's will for her. "Because I had been in one failed marriage, I carefully laid my heart open to the Lord, asking that He screen all of the men that I had an interest in and only allow the one person that He would choose for me into my life. I was comfortable by myself and was not out there looking for a relationship. I was explicit in what my expectations were and openly discussed those expectations with the people in my life. I allowed myself to consider a relationship only when it was obvious that the person met all of those expectations." Believing that she had met the right person, Dee got married again and had two children from this union.

After about eight years, it became obvious that she was living a lie. The person she had married did not really exist. She found out that he had concealed who he really was, being careful to show her only the parts of his life that fit her expectation of him. The real person had little fear of God and was actually involved in things that Dee could not be a part of, things that were dangerous for her and their children. With a sense of despair, Dee watched her second marriage fall apart and all she could do was ask the same questions she had asked before. "Lord, what did I miss?"

SECTION REVIEW

1. Dee's question, "Lord what did I miss" highlights the fact that young people often get married without noticing potential problem areas. Make a list of six to seven things that are easily missed during a courtship or dating relationship.

---

2. It is the little things that we often overlook during courtship that make or break a marital relationship. What are five of these often overlooked things that one should pay close attention to in a potential mate?

---

3. Make a list of people that are engaged in your congregation and in your immediate family. Write down any struggles that these people are currently facing, if any.

Take turns praying by name for these couples.

Although Dee's major in college was communication and public relations, it became obvious after graduation that her career path would take a completely different turn. Her first job was in a bank where she worked for twelve years, both as a credit investigator and a collection manager. When the career center closed down, Dee had no problem finding another job. She was becoming well-known as a hard worker who did her job well and she worked well with people. Almost immediately, she was employed by a non-profit agency as a volunteer manager. She was in charge of recruiting and managing volunteers for a youth development non-profit agency in the Nashville area, a job she enjoyed and became quite good at especially since she loved working with people.

The expertise she brought to the job led to the growth and expansion of the agency. Unfortunately like other institutions, the agency began feeling the brunt of the recession that hit the whole country in 2008 and so, to Dee's surprise, she was laid off from this job. Last hired, first fired. Losing this job at this time in her life, (right before Christmas) was a big test of her faith.

Being in a faith-based, non-profit agency, Dee had high expectations of the people she worked with and she recalls the morning she was laid off with mixed emotions. "It was on December 14th when I was called into the office by the director. He told me I had done a wonderful job with the agency, but that funding was becoming a problem and they had to let me go. Without any notice, whatsoever, I was told to go to my office, pack my bags that moment and leave. I remember asking incredulously, 'You mean, now?' The director confirmed that he wanted me to leave immediately." Dee admits that although this was said in a loving way, "It still hurt to the core. To make matters worse, the director asked the office manager to watch over me while I packed my things and took them out of the office."

Dee felt hurt and angry that her integrity was called into question. Over and over she questioned why God allowed this to happen to her. This job loss floored her. "I did not understand at all why God would allow somebody who had faith in Him; someone who had been living right; someone who was trying to raise her children right; someone who had honored him all her life and was already reeling from losses accompanying two divorces to go through this."

"Although what I was going through did not make sense, my mantra was to surrender all. Early in my life, my favorite song had been 'I Surrender All,' and at this difficult time in my life, I found myself learning to truly surrender to Him who knows it all. You see, I believe the key to surrendering all is not to begin surrendering when times are bad, but to build a continual relationship with God that will serve as a source of support when times get bad. It's not easy to learn to surrender in the middle of a great storm. Habit will make you hold on to something that makes you *feel* secure. Early on in your Christian walk, you have to learn to surrender."

Dee felt as if she had suffered a major blow, especially considering the timing of her termination. Little did she know that in just a few days she would actually be thanking God for being fired by that agency.

Realizing that her termination meant she would lose her health insurance by the end of the month, Dee made an appointment for her annual physical, which included a mammogram. The results of the mammogram would later reveal she had breast cancer. This was another terrible blow to Dee. The questions flooded her mind as she fell to her knees. Cancer? On top of everything else she had been through? "Why, Lord? Why?" She asked over and over. Although no answers came, Dee felt a strange sense of peace in the realization that God was still in control even though nothing made sense anymore. She immediately began an aggressive course of treatment. In the midst of the turmoil, Dee began to thank God for her termination by that agency, as that was what led to her getting a mammogram done at the time she did.

Now, after a double mastectomy and a series of chemotherapy treatments, Dee is living a life filled with joy and peace as she continues to raise her children in the Lord. She has become a successful author, a sought after speaker within the Nashville area and beyond, a living testimony to the faithfulness of a loving Heavenly Father. The journey has been a difficult one, but through it all, Dee has remained secure and steadfast, offering the following as the reasons why she is still standing:

a. Her church family. "I know without a doubt that I could not have made it without my church family. There are great brothers in the church, and I am very grateful for them, but what has made the greatest difference for me has been those that I call my sister posse. Everybody needs a sister posse—a small group of ladies that you can call on at any time—rain, snow, sleet, or hail, midnight or midday, and they will be there for you.

b. Friends beyond our church body. Often we hide behind the cloak of denominationalism and isolate ourselves from those who can help us the most. Not so for Dee. "I have never believed that my closest friends can only be members of my local congregation. While I am not Catholic, I will never forget one of my closest Catholic friends who lights a candle for me daily, and I know that God hears those prayers too."

c. A strong conviction that God will turn all things to His glory and to our good. As God's children, Dee is convinced that we will not always understand why things happen the way they do. "I do not fully understand why things happened the way they did in my life. Christians are often consumed with knowing God's will for their lives. Was it God's will that my marriages end in divorce or did the men in my life use their gift of freewill to make the wrong choices? I do not know the answer. But what I do know is that God will always work everything out for our good and for His glory."

d. God is big enough to handle our questions, doubts, and fears. "I have always been open enough to ask God, 'Why?' I go to Him when I am sad, confused, and angry, knowing not only that He will understand, but that he can handle all my emotions." She recalls telling a friend once that she was tired, and when the friend confused her being tired with her giving up, she told him that God understands it is possible to be tired, but still remain in the race. "I often get weary and tired, but I am in this race for the long haul. God has been faithful to me and even though I often have to lean my whole weight on Him, with His arms holding me close, my victory is assured."

e. The greatest legacy for a successful life is a foundation built on God and His faithfulness. Some people give up when life's troubles toss them to and fro, but not Dee. "My parents laid a solid foundation that is strong enough to help me face the storms of life. It is important that I model that foundation of strength for my children. If they can look back years from now and recall the days when I kept on keeping on, despite the pain and the hassle, it will all have been worth it."

f. The simple things in life bring the greatest joy. Dee is quick to laugh out loud at simple pleasures, claiming that sometimes we take life too seriously. Living in my own house, in spite of the fact that I have been out of a job for the past few years, hearing my children call out goodnight to each other at the end of a busy day, posting uplifting messages on Facebook, and reading uplifting messages from friends, these are the things that make life worth living."

Section Review

4. Dee is a strong advocate of "sister posse" to see us through dark and dreary periods in our lives. List those who would make up your "sister posse" group. Write a letter of gratitude to each of them today.

_____

_____

_____

5. Someone in your local congregation or in your sphere of influence needs a sister posse today. Ask the Spirit of God to lead you to a special person whose life you can touch by simply being there for them today. Write down the person(s) He places on your heart today.

_____

_____

_____

6. Which of the above strategies for helping Dee stand strong would be most useful in helping you hold on through days of pain and sorrow and why?

_____

_____

_____

CHAPTER 10

Achi - brim [Laugh at Me No More]

One of the great benefits of having a strong faith is that one no longer needs to have a sense of being totally in control. You begin to relax in the fact that your Father in Heaven is fully in control and that today's tears will lead to a glorious tomorrow. Making the right choices simply align you more closely to His will for your life, for as a good Father, He has great plans for us all.

—Uduak Afangideh

THE NIGERIAN CIVIL War, like any other war, had its share of deaths, heartbreaks, and despair. Although Grace Thompson was not alone in facing the distress associated with the awful Biafran war, it almost felt as if her world had come to an end. It was barely a week since the Biafran soldiers had marched into her compound, killed her husband, and took her ten-year-old son away as a prisoner of war. The compound was now deserted. The other wives had run off with their children to a safer part of the state, but she refused to leave. It wasn't that she had nowhere to go. She was a princess of the nearby Ngwa village, but the thought of leaving her matrimonial home for any reason was unthinkable. As she sat alone in the church building next to her family compound, her life flashed before her eyes and the past few days seemed more of a dream than reality.

She had been only a teenager when she was given in marriage to a man from her own *Igbo* tribe. Being the first daughter of a chief, the *Ada Eze*, the marriage was arranged and was celebrated with all the pomp and pageantry of a royal wedding. She was a good and dutiful wife, but after giving birth to two children, a girl and a boy, she could no longer endure the hardships of an abusive relationship. The marriage was dissolved by her husband's death, and Grace was left alone to raise her children.

Sometime thereafter, on a visit to her cousin in the nearby village of Ikot Ineme, she met and fell in love with T. A. Ideh. Theirs was a love marriage in the 1940's, a time in Nigeria where arranged marriages were the norm. Although he was from a different tribe, he too was of royal lineage and so the two families were overjoyed by the union. Grace gladly moved across tribal and state lines and established her matrimonial home in her new village. Despite reassurances by her husband, Grace became despondent when the first two years passed and she was unable to have a child. After five years of an infertile marriage, she became a source of ridicule in a society whose general belief was that a wife's primary duty was to give birth to sons who would become heirs and successors of their father.

Grace knew that the only way to fulfill her obligation to her marital family was to convince her husband to marry another wife, one who would bear the children that she could not bear. Since polygamy was an acceptable part of the Nigerian culture, and a sign of a man's influence and prestige, her husband married three other wives and became the father of many children. Being the first wife in a polygamous marriage had a few privileges, and Grace became an honorary mother to all the children. She was given the title *Nne* which is loosely translated as "mother of all." Being childless in her second marriage did not result in bitterness, but Grace settled down to raising her stepchildren, along with their mothers, in the fear of God. She quickly settled into the role of a matriarch in her extended family of marriage.

SECTION REVIEW

1. Grace's second marriage resulted in her being part of a blended family. What are some difficulties that arise in blended families?

_____

_____

_____

2. What specific steps can be taken by a step mother who desires to assist in raising her step children in a way that glorifies God?

_____

_____

_____

3. Because of her strong in faith in God, Grace's barrenness was not a source of bitterness to her. What are some Bible passages that could bring comfort to those who need to trust God when it appears that the desires of their hearts are not granted?

_____

_____

_____

4. Grace or Nne (as she was more commonly called) became a source of ridicule in her community because of her barrenness. What causes women to be ridiculed in our society today and what are some negative ways of dealing with such ridicule? What are some positive ways of dealing with such ridicule?

_____

_____

_____

5. Pause and say a prayer for a lady that you may know who appears to be shunned or who feels alone because of what she is going through. In what ways can you reach out to her this week?

_____

_____

_____

Nne was an industrious woman, a hardworking farmer, and a successful trader who traveled far distances to various village markets to sell her wares. She was respected far and wide and became a woman leader among the Igbo and Annang women of her community. Growing up at a time when Nigeria was chafing under British rule, Nne became involved in various political changes in the southeastern region of Nigeria. She was only nineteen years old when Nigerian women protested against taxation of female traders resulting in the Aba Women's riot of 1929. As a result of the protests, the position of women in the Nigerian society was greatly improved. When the success of the Aba riot led to other protests by women, Nne was one of the leaders of the protests that took place among Ngwa and Annang women in 1938.

Nne was comfortable in her childlessness, not knowing that God had other plans for her. In 1956, at the age of forty-six, Nne became pregnant. This coincided with the time that her daughter from her first marriage was also nursing a baby. Not only was Nne shocked at the prospect of being a mother and a grandmother at the same time, she was again ridiculed by the people of the village who were convinced she was too old to be having a baby. Nne recalled literally moving into the church building during the pregnancy of her son. "I knew that this pregnancy was a gift from God. Although the risk of giving birth to a baby that late in life was high, I was confident that God would see me through."

The taunts of the village women would ring in her ears as she went about her daily duties. Their famous taunt was a Nigerian saying to the effect that when the snail is ready to die, it lays eggs. "I knew they were predicting that my pregnancy this late in life would have dire consequences, but my faith was in a God who could do all things, and I knew that He would see me through. My solace was found in God and I took refuge in His house, virtually living in the church building until my delivery."

For Nne, one of the great benefits of having a strong faith was that she did not need to feel that she was in control. It became easier for her to realize that her Father in Heaven was fully in control and she believed strongly that the tears she cried daily would lead to a glorious tomorrow. Her faith was rewarded as she gave birth effortlessly to a baby boy, whom she fondly called, *"Ebe Nne."* Two years later, she became pregnant again and gave birth to another son, whom she called, *"Nwulu,"* an Ibo name for a second son. She had established her rightful position in her husband's household, not just because she was the first wife, but she was now a mother of sons. These sons brought tremendous joy to Nne, her husband, and the entire household. They were extremely bright, excelling in school, confident in parents who loved them and who would spare nothing to give them the best that life could offer.

SECTION REVIEW

6. The words of a Nigerian song "nkpo akanam mmi mfehe ndiwanga fi-o, Andiwam," describes one whose problems drive her to fall at the Lord's feet and hold on to His ankles in desperation. This was Nne's frame of mind when she moved into a church building for the duration of her pregnancies. What is that situation in your life that is driving you to seek solace in Him alone Who can solve every problem? Take time to write down your petition to the Lord, trusting that He who promised is faithful (see 1 Peter 5:7; Hebrews 10:23).

_____

_____

_____

7. Read 2 Chronicles 20:1-23 and note the theme that the battles we face belong to the Lord and He alone will ensure our victory. What battle are you currently facing?

_____

_____

_____

8. Just like Jehoshaphat in the above story, write a prayer below in which you hand over that battle to the Lord and stand by to see the victory that comes when all we can do is trust.

_____

_____

_____

Raising her children consumed Nne and she was almost oblivious to the major changes taking place in Nigeria's history. Like other African nations at the time, Nigeria was an artificial structure initiated by former colonial powers which had neglected to consider religious, linguistic, and ethnic differences. Nigeria, which gained independence from Britain in 1960, had at that time a population of about 60 million people consisting of nearly 300 different ethnic and cultural groups. The proclamation by the Igbo-dominated southeast, under Colonel Odumegwu Ojukwu, that the southeastern region would secede from Nigeria to become the Republic of Biafra, led to a declaration of war by the Nigerian government. While the people of the southeastern region supported the Biafran war, the lack of sophisticated weapons and trained soldiers was a big disadvantage and resulted in casualties among Biafran soldiers.

The civil war began in 1967 as the result of economic, ethnic, cultural, and religious tensions among the various peoples of Nigeria. Although Nne and her family lived in the Biafran region, her husband did not believe in armed conflict, so he focused on keeping his family safe and secure, praying that the war would soon come to an end.

Reality hit hard as Nne recalled the events of the previous week with tears streaming down her face. The day had started like any other day, except that for reasons she did not initially understand, her youngest son had stayed unusually close to his father all day. There had been whisperings and meetings on the front porch of their house, but Nne left such worries to the men and focused on household duties in the kitchen and the backyard.

She recalled the troop of soldiers that marched into the compound, without any warning, and the screams as the children and others ran in terror. She and the other wives fled into the house and locked themselves inside one room, praying for safety, unaware of the massacre that was taking place under their noses. She later found out that at the approach of the soldiers, all of the people in their large compound had fled the scene except for her ten-year-old son who followed close behind as the soldiers took her husband to the church building next door.

The church was built on land donated by her husband, and he had preached and been a leader of that church for many years. She was not surprised that when it became obvious that the Nigerian soldiers who invaded the compound came for his life, he asked to be allowed a final moment in the church building. Hours later, the village was silent, the soldiers had gone, having looted and stolen from the homes of the villagers, leaving carnage and destruction behind them.

Nne wailed with the other members of the family at the sight of her husband's dead body, but her tears turned to numbness and shock when she realized that her ten year old had been taken as a prisoner of war. She was inconsolable, not only at the death of her husband, but at the fact that it was at the same time as the loss of her son. This grief was more than she could bear, especially as she recalled her years of childlessness and the heartaches accompanying those years. How could a loving God give her laughter in her old age, and then rip her heart out?

Slowly, the numbness wore off, a funeral service was conducted for her husband T. A. Ideh, and the whole village mourned him for days.

Eventually life returned to its fearful normalcy for other members of the household, but Nne did not know where to find the strength to go on. Having lost the head of the family, the large extended family began disintegrating. The two other wives thought it best to return with their children to their various families of birth where family members would provide much needed financial and moral assistance.

SECTION REVIEW

9. The Word says in Proverbs 10:22 that the blessing of the Lord makes rich and He adds no sorrows. Often, though, the things that God blesses us with also seem to bring us heartaches and pain. Make a list of God's blessings and the things that accompany them which appear to cause more sorrow than joy.

_____

_____

_____

10. How do we reconcile the fact that a loving God allows bad things to happen to His children? What are current examples of bad things happening to some good people that you know?

_____

_____

_____

Nne could not fault their decision as she watched the wives pack and leave, but she could not find it in her heart to leave her matrimonial home. She knew it would be tough to live the life of a widow in a village torn apart by war and in a male-dominated society. But she felt deep in her heart that leaving Ikot Ineme would mean abandoning her husband and the love they had shared for many years. Nne recalls the morning she woke up with a renewed sense of resolve. "My heart was heavy, but my spirit was unbroken. I owed my husband something for the years we had spent together. I would not dishonor his memory by leaving and taking my son. I had to raise him the way his father would have wanted and that could best be done by keeping him in his father's house. I knew that it would take more strength than I had, but I felt deep in my heart that God would give me the strength needed to do the right thing. Maybe everything I had gone through was to prepare me for this new path in my life."

Nne got up that morning, took her first son by the arm, and went to her farm for the first time in months. She knew she would grieve for a long time, but was determined to use that grief as an impetus for survival. She knew that the only way she could make it was to depend completely on the Lord. Nne spent every spare moment in the church building, either waxing the floors, sanding the clay-covered walls, removing weeds from the nearby bushes, or worshiping with songs of praise and cries of lament and loss.

She recalled a lady passing by one day while she was sanding the walls. The lady stopped and watched her for a long time and then with a loud sigh taunted her saying, "What reason do you have to still serve the Lord after all the troubles he has allowed in your life?" Nne recalled that the only answer she could give was, "I know God is faithful and right now, He is all that I have in a world that doesn't make sense anymore." She had endured the taunts of her village women before and she knew deep in her heart that one day their mockery of her would come to an end. She firmly believed that one day she would be the one to tell them "*Achi-brim*, laugh at me no more." She held on to her faith in God, believing like Job that she could not expect only good from the Lord, but was determined to serve Him in all circumstances.

SECTION REVIEW

11. Right after the brutal killing of her husband and the kidnapping of her son, Nne could not understand how a loving God could give her laughter in her old age and then rip her heart out. Share an incident in your life in which you felt that God's blessing was also the source of your sorrow.

   _____

   _____

   _____

12. Nne's decision to remain in her husband's house was an unpopular one and was different from what the other wives did. What makes it easy for us to stick with difficult decisions despite what others are doing?

   _____

   _____

   _____

13. Nne found solace in serving in God's house. What activities serve as balm to your aching heart?

   _____

   _____

   _____

The years slowly went by as the civil war dragged on, and in January 1970, the war ended almost as abruptly as it had begun. Nigerians far and near rejoiced that the brutality and carnage was over, but Nne felt that she had no reason to rejoice. Not only had she lost a husband to the war, she had no idea what cruel fate had befallen her baby boy. She believed that the soldiers had also killed him since she had no idea what had transpired after the murder of her husband. Rumors of prisoners of war being tortured and eventually killed by the Biafran army were widespread, but she held on to a thread of hope that maybe, just maybe, her son had been spared.

This hope had kept her praying daily for him, believing despite all odds that she would see him again. She held onto this hope even when there was no reason to hope, often reciting Hebrews 11:1 over and over to keep her from despair.

About a month after the war was over, Nne woke up one morning with a sense of anticipation that she had not felt in a long time. She recalled that her heart started beating rapidly upon awakening and the first thought that came to her mind was, "Faith is the evidence of things hoped for, the substance of things not seen." Not stopping to question why the verse from Hebrews 11:1 came to her mind without prompting, she started reciting it as she got up from bed and began her day, not knowing that was the day the heavens had chosen to reward her faith.

The day dawned like any other day, with chores and gardening, but around mid-morning, there was a stir in the village. The voices of people shouting filtered in from the village square and for a community still suffering the aftermath of a violent war, it was uncertain if these were shouts of terror or of joy. Nne called her oldest son, and together they paused in their duties and listened. As the shouting grew louder and louder, it almost sounded as if she could hear her name being called out among the ruckus, so she inched a little closer to the edge of the family compound to see what was going on.

As she saw got close enough to see the crowd which was growing larger by the minute, Nne almost fainted with unbelief and shock, for lifted high above the crowd was her son who had been captured by the Biafran army and taken as a prisoner of war. Her son was returning home. She had dreamed of this day for so long that now she could hardly believe it was not still a dream. She almost fainted from relief and joy and had to lean on the person nearest to her. As he ran through the crowd and then held her tightly, their tears mingled. All she could say was "Nwulo, oh, Nwulo," calling him by the name she had affectionately given to him at birth.

She did not dare think of the horrors his young eyes had seen. All she allowed herself to do was praise God who had kept him safe throughout the war and had brought him home to her. As she watched him sleep that first night, Nne promised God that she would do all within her power to raise this son, who had been rescued from death, and his brother, to know Him and to be great vessels in His Kingdom all the days of their lives. Throughout the rejoicing and celebration of the next few days, Nne's heart was full of gratitude as she decided to put off her widow's garbs and live a life of rejoicing, for God had indeed proven Himself faithful.

With the return of her youngest son, the issue of his welfare and his education became a huge burden on Nne's heart and that of her oldest son. Although her late husband desired that his sons be fully educated, Nne's occupation as a subsistence farmer could not finance education for either of her sons. With a heavy heart she agreed, against both her and her youngest son's desire that he should become an apprentice to a merchant who sold clothes in the large Aba market. This meant that he would have to ride on his bicycle for miles daily from his village to Aba everyday to sell clothes and his pay would depend on his daily sales.

Although this was a tedious job for one so young, Nne was grateful that her son had a source of income that would not only keep him out of trouble, but would also assist in keeping the rest of the family clothed and fed. Every evening she would cry silently as she listened to his stories of gazing longingly at all the school children in their starched uniforms marching in through school gates, knowing that was a world he would never be part of. Nne's constant prayer was that God would miraculously change their fortune and make it possible for her son to go to school. She kept that constant prayer request between her and her God for fear that others would think it was a pipe dream.

Barely a year into his apprenticeship, Nne was approached by one of the elders of the village with an idea that appealed to her tremendously. In an attempt to empower local farmers, the Nigerian Government had instituted a program whereby people with a background in farming could be trained at an Agricultural Institute for three years and at the end of the training, would be given a grant to embark on medium scale farming in their locality. Nne immediately encouraged her youngest son to apply and tarried in prayer that his application be accepted. It was.

A few months later, she sent him off to Obio-Akpa, where the Agricultural Institute was located, grateful that her son was finally in school. Nne's joy could hardly be contained when after the first year, her son informed her that in addition to his studies at the Agricultural Institute, he was also studying for his high school general certificate examination, with a dream of going on to university. And then a few years later, he approached her one evening with an admission letter from the prestigious university of Lagos, Nigeria, to study law.

Nne grabbed him in a fierce hug, just knowing that her heart would burst with pleasure. Was this the son whom she had thought she would never see again? The son, whose future appeared bleak without a father to invest in his education? Her joy which knew no bounds was almost instantly replaced with dismay. How would they finance a legal education? Her oldest son had worked tirelessly to send this youngest one to the Agricultural Institute and to finance a higher school certificate, but they could not, in their wildest dreams afford a university education.

With a heartbroken cry, she pushed him away from her, unable to explain to him that as pleased with him as she was, his admission letter was useless. After all, university education was for the children of rich parents and she was just a struggling widow. Darkness crept into her soul as she spent the night in tears, petitioning God to intervene once again on her son's behalf.

Morning came and as her son came into her room and told her about an idea of how to finance his legal education, Nne realized again that God had answered her prayers. She held her breath as he left to put his plan into action, praying the whole time. The plan which was well received by the village leaders resulted in the setting aside of the 27th of December every year as a day that the whole village would come together and raise money to send her son to the University of Lagos. The village gladly embraced the idea of supporting the education of this young man and in 1983, the dream of the whole village was realized as her son walked down the stage and got his law degree, the first lawyer in the village and the first Christian lawyer in the whole country of Nigeria.

Section Review

14. During the years when her son was a prisoner of war, Nne relied on Hebrews 11:1 to keep her from worry and despair. The Bible is full of promises which we can claim as God's children. Ask the Spirit of God to lead you to a passage that speaks to your heart as you wait on the Lord. Write this passage below and memorize it as you wait to see God work through it to grant the desires of your heart (Psalm 37:4)

_____

_____

_____

15. Sometimes, interruptions of our plans are actually divine interventions. Nne thought that the Agricultural Institute would be the extent of her son's education, but God used it as a stepping stone to a legal education. What is going on in your life right now that appears to be an interruption or a detour?

_____

_____

_____

Hand over these detours to God today and trust Him to use it as a stepping stone in helping you achieve the great plans He has for you.

---

16. Nne put aside her pride and allowed God to use the village in the education of her son. In what ways has pride sometimes kept you from asking for help?

Nne knew that God had answered her prayers for her sons through the years but she felt that something was still lacking in the life of her second son. Her first son was happily married with children, and she nursed the dream of seeing her second son raising children of his own. She believed that after getting a degree, marriage would be the next thing on his mind, but she watched as he appeared too focused on his legal career to think of settling down. Barely two years after law school, he started his own private legal practice and that consumed him, but she never stopped praying that God would bring a Christian lady into his life, one who would love and encourage him in his Christian walk. And then one day, he brought a young lady to the family compound. Nne saw how he treated her and the love in his eyes and knew that this was the one. She prayed fervently that God would open her son's eyes as he had opened hers. To her delight, about a year after that first visit, she was at their wedding. Two years later, his first daughter was born and three years after that, his first son. As the baby boy was brought and placed in her arms, Nne lifted him up to the heavens and with tears streaming down her face she said in her native Igbo language, "*Achi brim.* All you who laughed at me and mocked me so many years ago, laugh at me no more. My God has been faithful to the very end. Laugh at me no more."

Nne lived to the ripe old age of 97 years. Desiring to be reunited with her husband and her Lord and Master, she drifted off to sleep in her own bed in 2004 surrounded by those whom God had used to wipe away her tears. Her life was a testimony of God's faithfulness, and the lessons learned from the way she lived her life include:

a. We live by the choices we make: Nne made many difficult choices in her life, beginning from marriage at an early age and the decision to stay in her marital home when she became a young widow. Those choices defined her and charted a course for generations to come. She became well respected in her husband's community and was given the title, Nne, which translates "mother of all."

b. God has a plan for us all. Sometimes, when the sky is cloudy and the days are dark, we do not understand what those plans could possibly be. Nne realized that one does not need to understand what God is doing to trust Him fully. All we can do is simply trust, especially during the dark days, and that act alone, aligns us more closely to His will for our lives. That act shows that we are willing to allow Him to direct our paths and ensures that only His good and perfect will be done in our lives.

c. Life is full of detours: It is easy to feel that the path we are on is the one that God will use to bless us. The events in Nne's life clearly point to the fact that life's paths often require a series of turns. We can choose to resist these detours or to embrace them, knowing that every turn is already determined and planned for by the One who knows where each road leads. A life of regret is most likely a life lived by resisting detours and desiring to stick to known paths. Nne believed firmly that the things that we see as interruptions are often divine interventions. If we only allow Him free reign, He has promised that all things will work together for our good (see Romans 8:28) and He is faithful in His promises.

d. Life was meant to be lived in community: Nne became a mother to all in her village, opening up her heart and her home to those who passed through, always ready to lend a helping hand. Her home beside the church building in Ikot Ineme village was used for church fellowship meals and meetings, and she financially supported the preacher and his family. She portioned her farm lands to widows and orphans in the community and at her funeral, the greatest tribute about her was the reading of the famous poem, "House by the Side of the Road."

There are hermit souls that live withdrawn
In the place of their self-content;
There are souls like stars, that dwell apart,
In a fellowless firmament;
There are pioneer souls that blaze the paths
Where highways never ran-
But let me live by the side of the road
And be a friend to man.

Let me live in a house by the side of the road
Where the race of men go by-
The men who are good and the men who are bad,
As good and as bad as I.
I would not sit in the scorner's seat
Nor hurl the cynic's ban-
Let me live in a house by the side of the road
And be a friend to man.

I see from my house by the side of the road
By the side of the highway of life,
The men who press with the ardor of hope,
The men who are faint with the strife,
But I turn not away from their smiles and tears,
Both parts of an infinite plan-

Let me live in a house by the side of the road
And be a friend to man.

I know there are brook-gladdened meadows ahead,
And mountains of wearisome height;
That the road passes on through the long afternoon
And stretches away to the night.
And still I rejoice when the travelers rejoice
And weep with the strangers that moan,
Nor live in my house by the side of the road
Like a man who dwells alone.

Let me live in my house by the side of the road,
Where the race of men go by-
They are good, they are bad, they are weak, they are strong,
Wise, foolish - so am I.
Then why should I sit in the scorner's seat,
Or hurl the cynic's ban?
Let me live in my house by the side of the road
And be a friend to man.

—Sam Walter Foss

CHAPTER 11

He Who Promised Is Faithful

With the Lord on our side, every adversity, every
failure, and every heartache, carries with it the
seed of an equivalent or greater benefit.

—Napolean Hill

IF BEING AN African-American child in America in the 21st
century has its share of challenges, one can only imagine the
heartache and turmoil associated with growing up as a black child
in the 1950's. As the second oldest of six children, Judy faced more
hardship in her childhood than most children face in a lifetime.
In addition to the scarcity of food and resources associated with
being part of a large family, one of Judy's earliest memories is that
of her mom being beaten severely by her father, almost every night.
With tears flowing down her cheeks, more than fifty years later,
she recoils slightly as she remembers her younger siblings hiding
under the large table in the main family room or under their beds
listening to the beatings.

"I hated those beatings, almost more than my momma did. I
wanted it to stop. I wanted him to stop, but I was too young to
make him stop."

Morning would eventually come and her mother would seemingly put the events of the night behind her, but Judy could not.

Playing the scene over and over in her mind, she blamed herself for not having the courage to stop him. She promised herself that the next time it happened, she would do something. Although she secretly prayed there would not be a next time, every night was filled with sounds of her mother's sobs as she was being beaten and abused by Judy's father. By the time Judy was twelve years old she had convinced herself that it was up to her to stand up to her father since nobody else would. She felt that if she didn't, he would kill her mother. Little did she know the extent of her father's violent streak.

"One evening, I watched him grab my mother and hit her. Suddenly, I lunged at him shouting that he should stop. Stunned, my father stopped and stormed out of the room, but before I knew what his plan was, he was back with a shotgun pointed directly at me. The look on his face left no doubt that he was planning to fire that gun. He could not believe I had dared to confront him and he was going to make sure I would never do that again."

Judy remembers her mother shouting at her to run out of the house, so she ran as fast and as far as she could, knowing that her life depended on it. She spent that night at a cousin's house, barely able to sleep, not knowing whether she would ever be able to go home again. Eventually, her father allowed her to return home, but things were never quite the same again in her household.

There was no doubt that Judy's father was mentally ill. One of the signs of such sickness was the diabolical plan that he had for his daughters, using them to make money from men who abused young children. When Judy turned thirteen, she knew that her father would try to do to her what he had done with her oldest sister, and so life became filled with horror and dread. When her father started calling her out to greet his male visitors, she knew what was coming and began hatching a plan to escape his devious plan. Judy never had an opportunity to put her escape plan into action because her father died shortly thereafter of gunshot wounds. She claims it was the first time in her life that she actually believed there was a higher power out there watching out for her.

With her father's death, her mother relocated with the children and started trying to make a better life for all of them. Although

Judy hoped that life would get better, such hope was quickly dashed. Without skill or training, her mother could not adequately take care of the children. She had to survive the only way she knew how and this meant forcing Judy into having sexual relationships with a man who was more than thirty years older than her just so he could provide money to take care of the family.

"When I ended up getting pregnant by this man, my mother turned against me, and I had no other choice but to move in with him. By the time I was pregnant with my second child, we got married."

Growing up in an abusive home, Judy had very low expectations of marriage. When her husband started beating her morning, afternoon, and evening, it was almost as if she had been expecting it. "I did not know any different. For me it was the norm. I almost expected him to beat me up, especially since he was more of a father-figure than a mate. He would beat me so badly that I would lose consciousness during the beating. I was always crying, wishing there was somebody I could talk to, somewhere I could find relief, but there wasn't. My mother had been abused and so her advice was that I should just endure it and try to be a better wife." Judy lived with this abuse for nineteen years and finally when her husband beat her with a double-barreled shot gun, she ran away and went to stay with a friend of her uncle's in Washington.

SECTION REVIEW

1. It is an established fact that abuse is a cycle and that children of abusive parents often end up in abusive relationships. Judy's situation is a classic example of this. Discuss some strategies that an abused person can take in an attempt at breaking a cycle of abuse.

_____

_____

_____

2. Judy endured abuse for many years, not having anyone to talk to. Carry out an internet search or invite a counselor familiar with domestic abuse experience to discuss signs of abuse and suggest strategies of how to be there for one who is abused. Write down some of the strategies discussed below.

_____

_____

_____

3. Which of these strategies are you able to use in an effort to make a difference in the life of one who is abused?

_____

_____

_____

Judy eventually got a divorce from her first husband, but after a few months in Washington, she returned to Birmingham. It appeared as if her abusive ex-husband had been waiting for her. Despite the divorce, he started threatening her again, and Judy thought that the only way she could get away from him was to re-marry. Predictably, this marriage did not last, and Judy found herself divorced again barely a year into her second marriage. She decided to raise her children on her own, but life as a single mother was very tough. She depended on the goodwill of family and friends and especially on the support of her baby sister who combined the roles of caretaker, adviser, and friend in Judy's life. Judy started going to church with her sister and her family, but admits there was still a void in her life.

Not knowing how to fill this void, she again fell into the trap of seeking a person to fill the emptiness that only God could fill. After dating for many years, she married again. Her new husband appeared to be the answer to her prayers for love and companionship.

"I was not used to anybody being there for me, but I finally found somebody who was. For the first few years of our marriage, I felt completely loved and cherished and thought he was all I needed. I no longer called upon God to solve my problems. My husband became my god. I depended upon him completely and slowly pushed God out of my life."

Judy felt that she could trust her husband like she had never trusted any other person, and they went into real estate ventures and built a business together. "Those were good days. My life seemed to have gone from rags to riches. Our business was doing well and life was great. At least that was what I thought, not knowing I was living a false dream."

For the first five years of marriage, Judy had believed that her husband was completely faithful to her and that formed the basis of her trust and dependence on him. To her greatest dismay, she recalls the day she was informed by a close friend that her husband had been seen around town with another woman. She refused to believe it at first, but started following him discreetly. One day, she saw them together and it was obvious that he was involved in an adulterous relationship. The sense of betrayal was almost more than she could handle. Those first few days after Judy found out were the worst days of her life so far. "Not even the beatings by my first husband could compare to the hurt and heartache that I felt at this betrayal. I had no expectations of my first husband, my only idea of marriage then was based on my parents' marriage and so I expected to be abused, but this husband had shown me so much love that I had come to expect it. The hurt was terrible, and I cried myself to sleep more nights than I can remember, often having many sleepless nights."

Confronting her husband only made matters worse and Judy decided to confront the lady involved. Without disclosing her intentions to anyone, Judy confronted her husband's girlfriend with the intent of asking her to leave him alone for the sake of their marriage. What she had planned as an innocent confrontation led to Judy being arrested for attempted murder. She found herself in a court of law, arraigned before a judge, and her plea of innocence seemed to fall on deaf ears, especially when her own husband testified against her! She could hardly believe it when he took the witness stand and agreed with his mistress that she had planned to kill her for having an affair with her husband.

"It was as if scales were falling from my eyes. I immediately became aware of the fact that my love and loyalty had been misplaced. I felt that I could not even call on God to help me for I had betrayed Him by placing my husband above my Lord and Savior. I could not believe God would ever forgive me or be willing to take me back as His child."

Feeling completely bereft and alone, Judy would cry out for mercy to a God who alone could help her, hardly believing that He would. She had reached the depths of her despair and had nowhere to turn. "It was hard for me to believe that God could still love me in spite of myself and all the mistakes I had made. Slowly, however, I began to feel His arms of love around me. I knew my sister was praying for me and instead of a sense of condemnation, I began to feel an inner peace that I had never known. I felt God's love and I knew that no matter how the situation turned out, He would never let me down. On the day of my sentencing, I went in fearing the worst, but God turned things around for me."

Instead of being sentenced to a two-year imprisonment term that her lawyer had been preparing her for, Judy walked out of that courtroom a free woman. She believes that her life changed from that day forward. "I had wandered far from God, but from that day on, I began my journey back. I knew it would be a difficult journey, but I also knew it would be worth it. God had proven again that no matter how far we stray, He is always there, just waiting to receive us with open arms."

SECTION REVIEW

4. Many people seem to depend on God when life is difficult, but turn away from Him when the going is good. Judy admits to making her husband a god, thinking she did not need anything

or anyone else. Is there anything or anyone in your life that you are placing above God right now?

_____

_____

_____

5. What are some signs of such misplaced trust and loyalty?

_____

_____

_____

6. Sometimes it takes a terrible turn of events to turn people back to God. In Judy's case it took her husband's unfaithfulness and betrayal. Share some situations in your life that have been painful, but have brought about a turning point in your relationship with the Lord.

_____

_____

_____

7. I often fall and stumble and it is easy to feel sometimes that I have wandered too far from God to ever be loved again or trusted again by Him. The story of the prodigal son is a beautiful story of a faithful father lovingly receiving a son that has disappointed and failed him. Read this story in Luke 15:11-32 and then write a prayer of thanksgiving for God's faithfulness even when we turn our backs on Him.

_____

_____

_____

As part of her gratitude to God for His mercies, Judy extended the forgiveness she had received from God to her husband. She moved back in with him and tried to put the past behind her. They both worked hard at restoring trust and loyalty in their marriage, but this was short-lived as he died two months later. As Judy grieved his death, she was thankful that she had gone back to him and been a good wife to him till the end.

Life as a widow brought more than its share of expected grief to Judy. During the ten years of their marriage, she and her husband had made joint investments and these investments were bringing in great returns. Without giving her the time she needed to grieve, as soon as the funeral was over her stepchildren accused her of killing their father and sued her for everything.

While the estate was still being disputed, Judy fell into a bout of depression which lasted for years. Not being able to manage the investments, she lost everything, including her home. As the depression worsened, she could no longer take care of herself and had to move in first with her daughter and then with her sister. "I would sit in a darkened room for days just staring at the wall, not wanting to live. I felt that I had nothing to live for, I cried out to the Lord, but I could not hear Him answering me. Life was no longer worth living. I think everything I had been through since my childhood finally caught up with me and I no longer had the strength to carry on."

As a child, Judy had been searching for the Lord, going to different churches but not really finding a niche. In her late thirties she gave her life to Jesus and although she made some strides spiritually, it appeared she was consistently making wrong choices. At this darkest point of her life, the church became her refuge—the one place she could go to and find peace. She says that moving in with her sister was the best decision she ever made. "She was my baby sister and I hated to burden her with my problems, but I had nowhere else to go. I had lost my business, my home, and my health, and I was afraid I was losing my life. I had nowhere to go. My sister took me in and saved me."

Although Judy's sister was a single mother of two girls, her lifestyle had a stability that Judy's lacked. She was an active member of the Lord's Church, teaching classes, serving the Lord faithfully, and modeling for her daughters what a godly woman should be. She immediately embraced the challenge of helping Judy put her life back in order, helping her set healthy boundaries for herself and establish a set of priorities in which God was front and center of everything. Within a couple of years, things turned around for Judy. "I started reading the Word as I had never read it before and I found peace for my soul. My faith started to increase and I began to depend only on God to see me through."

She reclaimed one of the buildings that she had bought with her husband, turned it into a business, and slowly began to make it an income-generating venture. Today, Judy is living in her own home, holding her head up high, knowing that she is making it only by the grace of God. Some of the main lessons from Judy's life are:

a. The things you face as a child do not define who you are destined to become. Too many children who face difficult situations believe that there is no way out of those situations and so they do not even try to make something better of themselves. Judy grew up with an abusive father and then got herself into an abusive marriage, but she believed that life was meant to be better; so she kept searching. Her belief that it is possible to dust oneself off and try again has helped her live a life of victory instead of defeat.

b. Family will always be there for you. Judy admits that her life would not have dramatically changed for the better if not for the love of her sister. Together, they are like two peas in a pod. "Even though, she is my younger sister, her faith in me has inspired me to believe in myself. She has often been strong when I have been weak and I have often leaned on her strength and allowed her to carry me." Often, sisters grow up and grow apart, but Judy believes what Barbara Alpert wrote about sisters: "She is your mirror, shining back at you with a world of possibilities. She is your witness, who sees you at your worst and best, and loves you anyway. She is your partner in crime, your midnight companion, someone who knows when you are smiling, even in the dark. She is your teacher, your defense attorney, your personal press agent, even your shrink." She urges us all to draw close to our sisters, whether they are birth sisters or faith sisters.

c. You can never fall too far from God's grace. Judy went through a season of her life when she believed she had turned her back on God one time too many. She was so sure He would never forgive her, even when, like the Prodigal Son, she longed to be taken back as a servant. She found out that we can never stray so far that God's love and grace cannot reach us. No matter how badly we treat Him, He is always ready to forgive, take us back as sons and daughters, and wipe the slate clean. This realization changed Judy's life. When she accepted God's forgiveness, she learned not only to forgive herself, but to forgive others who had hurt and betrayed her. Today, she tells the youth groups and women's groups that she speaks to about the joy and freedom that comes from accepting forgiveness so that one can easily forgive others.

d. God is faithful, no matter what. Like a loving father, He has wonderful plans for all of His children, and when we mess up and suffer the consequences of our mess, He will always be there. When we suffer in abusive relationships or as a result of other people's messes, He is still faithful and will always make a way for His children.

Judy's advice is to, "Believe that God loves you and will hold on to you, never to let go. I often wanted to kill myself when I was going through my mess, but today, I thank Him that He not only saw me through the mess, He used my mess to draw me closer to Him and make me who He wanted me to be. Keep the focus on Him, and He will change things around for you."

CHAPTER 12

The Peace That Comes From Knowing That God Is Always There

The two most powerful warriors are patience and time.

—Leo Tolstoy

IN TODAY'S WORLD, it is rather unfortunate that growing up with parents who are divorced seems to be the norm. This was not the case when Jay was growing up in the 1960's. Her parent's divorce was, however, only one of the challenges that Jay faced in her childhood years. Her father's job as a construction worker meant living a nomadic life and her earliest memories are those of traveling with her family wherever her dad's job took him, living in a travel trailer, bathing in community showers, and living a communal lifestyle with families of the other construction workers. This lifestyle continued until her parents divorced when she was nine years old and resulted in Jay growing up without much of the stability that a young child craves.

Prior to the divorce, Jay recalls that her father was into drugs, and this nightmare became part of the reality of her childhood years. She remembers walking into their storage shed one day and observing with childlike wonder the plants that her father was nursing in the shed, not knowing they were marijuana. It seemed as if everyone in the tiny community they lived in was growing marijuana. "I remember a personal visit to the houses in our neighborhood one evening by a deputy sheriff with the information that there would be a raid the next day so that the marijuana growers could hide any evidence of their drugs. I thank God that my mother, knowing what it would do to us, moved us out of that environment."

The divorce led to her mom moving to Alabama so the children could be closer to their grandparents, and this proved to be just what the young children needed. Determined to raise the children properly, Jay's mom bought a house and started working. Loneliness and the challenges of being a single mother of three young children drove her quickly into a couple of other failed marriages before she realized that she did not need a man in her life to be happy.

Those years of watching her mom suffer from one terrible marriage to another made an impression on Jay and she resolved to always stand on her own and not depend on someone else for her sense of self worth. By the time she was in junior high, she had decided to do whatever it took to make it on her own and to never depend on a man, either emotionally, financially, or otherwise.

SECTION REVIEW

1. The percentage of children growing up amidst drugs and alcohol has increased over the years. What can the Church as a body do to reach out to these children?

_____

_____

_____

2. There is a current debate about legalization of marijuana. Carry out an internet search on the pros and cons of this debate. Sample the opinions of family members and church members

and then write down your own views and your reasons for those views below.

_____

_____

_____

3. Divorce has devastating effects on the adults involved, but also on the children. Write down some of these effects and some things that can be done to reduce the severity of those detrimental effects.

_____

_____

_____

4. Many psychologists suggest that women should wait for one to two years after a divorce before dating again and definitely before marrying again. Would you agree or disagree with this suggestion? State reasons for your answer.

_____

_____

_____

Jay's desire for independence drove her to succeed in whatever she did and led to her graduating as salutatorian of her class and getting a scholarship to go to college. No one in her family had ever gone to college, and although her mother supported her decision, Jay was completely on her own financially. Jay's scholarship was for the local community college, but she wanted to leave that small community, so she decided to go to college in the nearby city of Troy, Alabama. Although this meant that she would have to pay her own way through college, she was resolved to do whatever it took to make that happen.

Her first year in college, in a new environment and completely on her own, was eye opening for Jay. Although she learned a lot academically, she enjoyed her freedom to the maximum and by the middle of her first semester she realized that she did not like the person she was becoming. The challenges of her childhood had given her an uncanny ability to detach herself from her immediate environment and make objective judgments about what was going on around her. Thus, in the middle of a lifestyle of partying and drinking with her roommates and other college friends, she was able to see herself heading towards disaster.

"I saw that I was losing control fast and decided that I needed a stricter form of discipline for my life. So, I joined the army. The boot camp experience and the other forms of training brought me to my senses faster than anything else could have done at the time. When I returned to college, I was a completely different person—disciplined and focused and able to graduate from college at the age of nineteen."

The challenges that Jay faced would have been easier to bear if she had been introduced to God at an early age. She recalls living across from a Baptist Church and seeing people going in and out of the church even though she was not going to church herself. In her junior year, she got baptized, but she never felt that she belonged in church.

"The people always appeared hypocritical, and I could not understand why there were so many different churches, all of them claiming to be the right church. The people I met during military training seemed to be more authentic Christians, and I encountered God through interacting with these people more than by going to formal worship. I read my Bible and prayed regularly, but I did not believe in going to church."

This all changed in her junior year in college when she met a young man whose Catholic faith was important to him. They became close and when they began dating, Jay started going to catechism classes and learning a lot about the Catholic Church and also about organized religion.

After being in a relationship for five years, they started making plans for spending the rest of their lives together. He was from

Arizona, and they planned to live there to be near his family, and so two days after Jay graduated from college, she moved to Arizona. Jay believed that her future was well planned out, so could not believe it when what she had seen as a bright future came crumbling down around her feet.

After living in Arizona for six months, it was revealed to her that this guy was the wrong person for her. "I did not have a firm belief in a God that watched over me, but the circumstances surrounding my break up with this guy made me realize for the first time that my life was directed by a power higher and greater than me."

After the break-up, Jay returned to Alabama and began focusing on making a life for herself. She knew there was a lesson to be learned from her failed relationship and was resolved to move on. Early in her life, Jay had resolved that she would not make the same mistakes that the adults in her life had made. Now she felt that if she had been so wrong about a guy after knowing him for five years, it would be difficult for her to trust another person. She had a strong independent spirit, and although she dated and had a good social life she was wary of forming any kind of attachment to the guys she met.

After a few years, her best friend at the time, set her up on a blind date with a coworker of hers. Jay became attracted to the guy almost from the first date, but she was determined to turn him off by being at her worst behavior on subsequent dates. With a chuckle, she remembers how all her attempts failed.

"It still amazes me how he could see through my behavior to the person I was inside. He somehow knew that the foul language and questionable behavior was just an act and one day he called me out on it and said that he knew I was trying to scare him off, but that I would not succeed. He insisted that I accompany him to church, and our dates began to be centered on shared religious experiences.

"I knew almost immediately, that there was something different about this guy. He was genuine in his Christian walk, and for the first time I did not have the feeling that the Church was a place that I could never belong. I began to see it as a place where a group of genuine people were meeting together to seek how to please God.

I still had a lot of questions, so we studied the Bible together quite a bit. Slowly, I started wanting the kind of relationship with the Lord that I saw others have."

Jay believes that one of the reasons it took her so long to embrace Christianity was the divisiveness that she saw among Christians. "I met all these people going to different churches, claiming loudly that their religion was the best, but not able to articulate to me the reasons for their belief. I looked for ways that their religion made them different, but all I saw were similar lifestyles among Christians and non-Christians. Christians did not look happier or more peaceful because of their religion. I wanted more than what they had. I had no doubt in my mind that there was a God, but I wanted much more than what I saw around me. When I found it, I recognized it, and my life has never been the same since." Jay had a hunger for spiritual things which was slowly being satisfied as she began studying the Bible one-on-one with a Christian friend. She says that no one prior to this, had ever sought to help her find the answers to her questions by studying the Word. She claims that Christians would be more effective soul winners if we would point others to God's Word and allow God to speak for Himself.

Section Review

5. Jay says that the life-styles of Christians and non-Christians were not different enough to convince her that Christianity was essential to successful living. List the ways that Christians behave too much like non-Christians.

_____

_____

_____

6. One of Jay's virtues has always been the ability to dust herself off when life dealt unkindly with her and to be able to move on. Often it is easier to live in the past, agonizing over past mistakes, so afraid that we might repeat those mistakes that

we stay stuck in the past. Ask the Spirit to reveal to you the things that you are holding onto from your past. Write those things below, pray over them, and resolve to leave them in the past and move on. Read Paul's resolve in Philippians 3:12-14 and let this serve as your mantra to keep moving forward.

_____

_____

_____

Knowing the Lord on a personal level made a tremendous difference in Jay's life. She was able to forgive the adults in her life and gained renewed respect and admiration for her mother. She allowed the Lord to guide and lead every aspect of her life, so that when she fell in love this time, she knew it was for real. Within nine months of meeting the guy, she was married to him. Realizing that she had been in a five-year relationship that failed, Jay was initially surprised that just three months after meeting this guy, she knew he was the right person for her. "I think that studying the scripture with him and being led to the Lord by Him resulted in a deeper and stronger relationship. I knew he was genuine and that made it easy to fall in love with him. The Lord brought him into my life, and I thank Him for my husband daily."

Like many Christian women, Jay had to come to the point where she realized it was not her place to find the right person. She learned that God would lead her and she did not have to settle for the wrong person. Jay believes that trusting God to bring the right person into our lives will free us to do our part which is to live for Him, seek to please Him, and allow Him to do the rest. She believes that God's timing is always the best and we just have to trust Him to do what is right for us. "As Christian ladies, God desires to use us to raise the next generation of godly men and women for His Kingdom. He can only do that if He brings a godly man and a godly woman together. All that the young Christian lady has to do is seek His righteousness and He will bring the right person at the right time. This kind of mindset would alleviate the frustrations that accompany trying to find a Christian mate on one's own."

With the current generation recording the highest percentage of broken homes and failed marriages in history, Jay believes that parents need to be more intentional about praying for their children's future mates very early on. "I have very young kids but I pray daily that God will one day bring the right person into their lives; that He will be the one to choose who they spend the rest of their lives with. I am mindful that who they marry will determine forever the course of their lives. It will determine the simple decisions like where they live and complex ones like what they do for the Lord and for others. It is only the Lord who can make the right choices for them. We as parents can never start too early to pray for our children's future mates."

There seems to be vast research supporting the fact that children from broken homes tend to have failed marriages. Jay was mindful of this and resolved in her heart that she would not continue this cycle. "The person I married was important to me because I wanted to give my children the stability that I had lacked growing up. I pray daily for their future mates because it is important to me that they should have fulfilled marriages that will bring glory and honor to God in this messed up generation of theirs."

After three-and-a-half years of marriage, Jay found out that she was pregnant. She had just started graduate school, had her life well planned out, and a baby at that time was not part of the plan. Looking back, she is amazed at how God loves to surprise us by throwing a wrench into our well-laid plans. She became excited about the pregnancy, and the baby came just as she was wrapping up her graduate work. Three years later, she had a son, and raising her children became her greatest priority.

One of the greatest challenges in Jay's life came after the birth of her second child when just six months after he was born, she had a stroke. The doctors attributed it to a blood clot in her artery, and she remembers being terrified. "I was so grateful that I had known the Lord before this happened. The only prayers I seemed capable of praying were, 'Lord, my children have to have a mamma to raise them.' I knew deep in my heart that everything was going to be okay. I saw God step in, calm my fears, and arrange everything in a way that left no doubt that He was the one in control." Jay admits feeling closer to God during those days of uncertainty than she has ever felt.

Having open heart surgery was scary, but God arranged for a world renowned surgeon to perform the surgery, and nurses who understood her concerns and who were kind. Jay's recovery after the surgery was uneventful and rapid and she gives all the glory to the Great Physician Himself.

More than ten years after starting her family, Jay has made many major career changes. Her love for the Lord and for her family remains the constant in her life. As she looks back on her life, she shares these lessons learned from all that she has been through:

a. We must be able and willing to forgive and let go of our hurts. It would have been easy to blame her father for never being there for her, but Jay realized that holding a grudge against him would only wound her spirit. "As I matured in my spiritual walk, I realized that I am accountable to God for my actions and my reactions, and I made a conscious decision not to hold any grudge against my earthly father but to move on and live my life in a way that would please my Heavenly Father."

b. We should not allow our past to define who we are. Sadly, many children in this generation are growing up in broken homes, and it is easy to allow bitterness and anger to influence the decisions they make. It is easy for them to set limitations on themselves because of the things they lacked while growing up. Jay believes that such children must realize that they have a choice in who they turn out to be.

c. It is far too easy to wallow in regret and allow that to drag us down. Jay believes that "even though our past is a reality, we can make right choices that result in changing the course of our future. We must learn to control our circumstances, instead of merely reacting to them." Jay exemplified this in her own life when she chose the discipline of being trained in the military for a year instead of continuing with a riotous lifestyle in college. She lived out the maxim upon which this book is centered ... *we all live by the choices we make.*

d. We need to trust the Lord to direct our paths. Jay firmly believes that her life changed for the better when she came to know the Lord. She believes her husband was specially chosen for her by God as has been her career path. As long as we trust Him, He will surely direct our steps. He understands when we make mistakes. He knows that "we are but dust" and as long as we obey the conviction of the Holy Spirit, repent of our sins, trust His forgiveness, and dust ourselves off, He is faithful to forgive and to keep leading us.

e. No matter what happens, God is always there. Sometimes, going through difficult times makes us wonder where God is and why He allows so much pain. If we believe in His sovereignty and take the time to study His word, we will realize that His ways are not our ways, but that all things will work together for our good, as He has promised. When we feel far away from him, we should remember that He never moves and we should be willing to do whatever it takes to draw us back to Him.

f. We should not be quick to dismiss the hard times we face as those times might be personally designed to draw us closer to the divine. Having the stroke placed Jay in a position where she had to lean completely on the Lord. "I could not understand why this was happening at that time, but I had to trust that it did not take God by surprise. I spent more time talking to Him, listening to Him, and believing that He would lead us down the right path. I firmly believe that God often uses trials to lift us up to a higher plane where we can relate to Him as Lord and Master."

SECTION REVIEW

7. Jay believes that as young ladies, trusting God to bring the right person into our lives will free us to do our part, which is live for Him, seek to please Him, and allow Him to do the rest. State reasons why this is often hard for young ladies especially when they believe they are ready for marriage?

_____

_____

_____

8. What steps can we as Christian mothers take to drive the above thought home so that our children are convinced of its truth?

_____

_____

_____

9. Which of the lessons learned by Jay above is particularly needed by you in this season?

_____

_____

_____

APPENDIX

Resources to Assist in Establishing and Maintaining a Quiet Time With the Lord

THE CHALLENGES ONE faces when trying to establish and maintain daily quiet times with the Lord are actually finding the time to do it and deciding on how to do it. The one thing the women in this book have in common is that they carved out time to spend in God's presence and this singular action made the greatest difference in their lives. As you seek to develop this much needed discipline, it is important to decide on a specific time, find a quiet place, and have your Bible and notebook ready. The Lord of the universe will always be there to meet with you. Feel free to choose one or more of the books below to kick start your journey.

A Sunday Afternoon With the Preachers' Wives by Paula Harrington, Lulu.com, 2006.

A Woman After God's Own Heart by Elizabeth George, Harvest House Publishers, 2006

Be Still ... and Let Your Nail Polish Dry, Summer side Press, 2009.

Becoming the Woman I Want to Be by Donna Partow, Baker Publishing Group, 2004.

Desperate Christian Women by Sherry Debray, Tate Publishing & Enterprises, L.L.C, 2007.

Finding Calm in the Chaos: Christian Devotions for Busy Women by Kathleen Bostrom. Westminster John Knox Press, 2005.

Having a Mary Heart in a Martha World by Joanna Weaver, WaterBrook Press, 2000.

The Power of a Praying Woman by Stormie Omartian. Harvest House Publishers, 2007.

Woman, Thou Art Loosed! by T. D. Jakes, Baker Publishing Group 2007.

Made in the USA
Middletown, DE
24 January 2015